DICTIONARY
OF EMOTIONS

Words for Feelings, Moods, and Emotions

PATRICK MICHAEL RYAN

:-)-:

PAMAXAMA

Published by PAMAXAMA
All Rights Reserved.

:-)-: ®

Published in the United States.

ISBN: 0991359402
ISBN 13: 9780991359400
Library of Congress Control Number: 2014900226
PAMAXAMA, Portland, OR

INTRODUCTION

EMOTIONS ARE SUBJECTIVE. Emotions help define and communicate our internal and external condition and experience. *Dictionary of Emotions: Words for Feelings, Moods, and Emotions* is a collection of words to aid in recognizing, defining, and explaining one's own emotional experience.

The project started in 1989 when I was working full time as a professional actor. My passion for acting was anchored in exploring and experiencing emotion and the human condition. I found myself searching for tools to aid in improving both my characters' emotional development and my own emotional intelligence. I desired the ability to assign emotions and the intensity of those emotions to each circumstance in each scene of the script. This, I believed, would help me better understand the overall emotional experience of the character and the emotional arc of the story. I realized that a dictionary of emotions would be of value for all of us who want to expand our emotional vocabulary. With that in mind, I created *Dictionary of Emotions: Words for Feelings, Moods, and Emotions.*

This work serves as a tool for awareness and expression. I feel that it can be used to help us identify and understand many of our linguistic options for describing various states of our own emotional experience.

Due to the subjective nature of emotions, the meanings of the words are mostly short and concise. I have attempted to identify the core emotional essence of each word, leaving room for one's own interpretation, exploration, and expansion.

The definitions in *Dictionary of Emotions: Words for Feelings, Moods, and Emotions* represent common use of the words in the context of feelings, moods, and emotions. Many words have additional meanings, but for the purpose of this book, those definitions have been purposely left out.

I invite you to explore this book and to consider if you have ever described yourself as feeling...

abandon
Freedom from restraint or control; reckless freedom from inhibition or worry.

abandoned
Deserted or cast off.

abandonment
Emotional desertion or a feeling of separation from something.

abased
Shamed or humiliated from a degrading experience.

abashed
Embarrassed or ill at ease; self-conscious or ashamed.

abducted
Taken away by force and without consent.

aberrant
Markedly different from the norm or accepted standard.

aberration
Disorder in one's mental state.

abhor
Extreme hatred and/or disgust.

abhorred
Hated or detested.

abhorrence
Hate coupled with disgust.

abhorrent
Offensive to the mind.

ability
The quality of being able to perform; a quality that permits or facilitates achievement or accomplishment.

abject
Hopeless, without pride or dignity.

ablaze
Very excited (especially sexually).

able
Having the skill, know-how, or authority to do something.

abnormal
Different from what is normal, expected, or typical.

abominable
Exceptionally bad or displeasing; unequivocally detestable.

abominate
To hate in the highest degree.

abrasive
Sharply disagreeable; rigorous.

absolved
Free from guilt.

absorbed
Having one's complete attention or interest focused on someone or something.

absorbent
Having the power, capacity, or tendency to absorb or soak something up.

abstemious
Able to restrain oneself from consuming, doing, or enjoying something.

abstract
Existing only in the mind; separated from
embodiment.

abstracted
Lost in thought; showing preoccupation.

absurd
Inconsistent with reason, logic, common sense.

abulic
Characterized by an abnormal inability to act or make
decisions.

abundance
An overflowing fullness of something.

abused
Subjected to mental and/or physical cruelty or
mistreatment by someone or something.

abusive
Habitually violent and/or cruel.

abysmal
Extremely bad.

accelerated
Sped up, as of an academic course.

acceptable
Worthy of acceptance; satisfactory.

acceptance
Approval; favorable reception.

accepted
Recognized and approved of.

accepting
Tolerant without protest.

accessible
1. Easy to get along with or be spoken to; friendly.
2. Capable of being reached.

acclaimed
Praised and highly respected for something.

acclimated
Accustomed to a new environment or condition.

accommodated
Having one's needs met; welcome.

accommodating
Obliging; willing to do favors.

accomplished
Highly skilled at something, usually through education, training, and experience.

accomplishment
1. Something achieved.
2. An ability acquired by training.

accosted
Approached and/or spoken to aggressively.

accountable
Responsible and liable; able to answer to someone or something.

accredited
Officially approved; recognized.

accurate
Conforming exactly or almost exactly to fact or to a standard.

accusatory
Feeling as if another person has done something wrong.

accused
Blamed for a crime or misdeed.

accusing
Blaming someone or something for a crime or misdeed.

acerbic
Sarcastic and/or bitter about someone or something; harsh or corrosive in tone.

ache
Desire for something or someone who is not present; physical pain.

aching
Desiring something or someone who is not present.

acid
Harsh or corrosive.

acknowledged
Accepted and/or recognized.

acquiescence
Acceptance without protest.

acquiescent
Willing to carry out the orders or wishes of another without protest.

acquisitive
Eager to acquire and possess things, especially material possessions or ideas.

acrimonious
Strongly resentful or cynical.

activated
Ready for or put into motion.

active
Full of activity or engaged in continuous activity.

actualized
Making something real or concrete; give reality or substance to.

adamant
Impervious to pleas, persuasion, requests, or reason.

addicted
Dependent on something.

addled
Mixed up or confused.

adept
Knowledgeable, skillful, and apt.

adequate
Sufficient and/or acceptable.

admirable
Deserving of the highest esteem or admiration.

admiration
Delighted approval and respect.

admire
To have pleasure and/or wonder with approval and/or respect of a person, quality, or thing.

admired
Respected and approved of by someone.

admonished
Warned with an impression of punishment, causing one to feel on guard.

adorable
Lovable and/or very attractive.

adoration
Profound love and admiration.

adore
To love someone or something intensely.

adored
Deeply loved.

adorned
Beautified by something.

adrift
Lost and confused; without purpose or intention.

adroit
Skillful or adept in action or thought.

adroitness
Skillful performance or ability without difficulty.

adult
Fully developed; mature.

adulterated
Mixed with impurities; corrupt.

advanced
Further along than most people in physical or mental development.

adventurous
Willing to take risks and/or undertake or seek out new and daring experiences.

adversarial
Characterized by conflict or opposition.

adverse
Opposite or opposing of something.

aesthetic
Concern or appreciation for the visual characteristics of something.

affable
Diffusing warmth and friendliness toward others.

affected
1. Influenced by something.
2. Emotionally or cognitively impacted by someone or something.

affection
Positive liking for someone or something.

affectionate
Warm tenderness or fondness.

affinity
A natural attraction or kinship.

affirmative
Praise or approval of someone or something.

affirmed
Supported and encouraged.

afflicted
Mentally and/or physically unfit.

affluent
Financially well-off.

affronted
Treated or spoken to rudely by another.

aflutter
Excited with anticipation.

afraid
Fearful and apprehensive.

against
Opposing someone or something.

agape
1. Selfless love for another without sexual implications (especially love that is spiritual in nature).
2. Shocked or surprised.

aggravated
Annoyed, provoked, or incited (especially deliberately) to anger.

aggressive
Determination and energetic pursuit to achieve one's goal.

aggrieved
1. Treated unfairly; offended.
2. Sorrowful from a loss.

aghast
Struck with fear, dread, or dismay.

agile
Quick and light in thought, movement, or action.

agitated
Troubled or nervous.

aglow
Radiant; vivacious and happy.

agnostic
Doubtful and uncommitted.

agog
Excited by eagerness and/or curiosity.

agonize
To suffer from worry about something.

agonized
In great pain.

agony
Intense suffering.

agoraphobic
Abnormally afraid of open or public places.

agreeable
Willing to agree; pleasant or enjoyable.

ahead
Further along in time, process, or other measurements.

ail
To feel unwell or troubled.

ailed
Sick, indisposed, or troubled by something.

ailing
Somewhat ill or prone to illness.

aimless
Having no purpose or direction.

airy
1. Unconcerned about something that is typically taken seriously by others; nonchalant.
2. Elegantly and gracefully light.

alarm
Surprise and fear resulting from the sudden awareness of danger.

alarmed
Experiencing a sudden sense of danger.

alert
Perceptive and responsive.

alien
Foreign to a particular environment or experience.

alienated
Withdrawn, isolated, estranged, or dissociated.

alive
1. Full of life and spirit.
2. Alert, active; animated.

allegiance
Loyalty and commitment to an individual, group, or course of action.

alleviation
The feeling that comes when something burdensome is removed or reduced.

allied
Connected or joined by treaty or agreement.

allowed
Free to do something with permission.

allured
Feeling a powerful temptation from pleasure or advantage.

alluring
Highly attractive and able to arouse hope or desire.

almighty
Godlike with unlimited power.

alone
1. Isolated from others.
2. Exclusive of anyone or anything else.
3. Radically distinctive and without equal.

aloof
Distant, unfriendly, and unsympathetic.

altruistic
Unselfishly concerned for the welfare of others.

amateur
Lacking professional skill or expertise; inexperienced.

amazed
Overwhelmingly surprised, astonished, or shocked.

amazement
Extreme surprise or wonder.

amazing
Surprisingly great.

ambiguous
Open to more than one interpretation; uncertain.

ambitious
Strongly desiring success or achievement.

ambivalent
Uncertain or unable to decide what course to follow.

ambushed
Attacked without expectation.

amenable
Open and responsive to influence; easily persuaded or controlled.

amiable
1. Warm, friendly, and ready to please.
2. Disposed to please; good-humored.

amity
Friendship and cordiality.

amorous
Feeling sexual desire.

amused
Pleasantly occupied, entertained.

amusement
Delight at being entertained.

amusing
Entertaining to others, usually through humor and/or wittiness.

analyzed
Carefully considered or examined for something specific.

anarchistic
Disregarding laws and societal norms and believing in the absence of authority.

anchored
Firmly affixed to something; stable and grounded.

anemic
Lacking vigor or energy.

anesthetized
Unconscious or numb from an administered drug.

anger
A strong negative feeling that is oriented toward some real or supposed grievance.

angry
Strongly annoyed, displeasured, or hostile.

angst
Deep anxiety, usually about the world or about personal freedom.

angsty
Experiencing acute but unspecific anxiety.

anguish
Extreme mental distress.

anguished
Experiencing intense pain, especially mental pain.

anhedonic
Unable to experience pleasure.

animated
Full of life, lively; excited and expressive.

animosity
Ill will arousing active hostility.

annihilated
Completely destroyed.

annoyed
Aroused to impatience, irritation, or anger.

annoyance
Irritation or displeasure.

annoying
Troublesome and/or irritating.

anonymous
Unknown; without identity.

antagonistic
Arousing animosity or hostility.

antagonized
Treated with hostility.

anticipation
Foreseeing, forestalling, or preparing for something in advance.

anticipative
Eagerly expecting.

antipathy
Intense dislike.

antiquated
Obsolete or old-fashioned.

antisocial
Having no desire for the company of others.

antsy
Nervous and unable to relax.

anxiety
Worry and nervousness.

anxious
1. Eagerly desirous.
2. Fearful, uneasy, and worried.

apart
Having characteristics not shared by others; separate.

apathetic
Feeling no emotion or having a lack of interest; indifferent.

apathy
A lack of enthusiasm for or interest in things generally.

apologetic
Regretful of having caused trouble for someone.

appalled
Horrified; struck with fear or dread.

appealed to
An earnest request from somebody.

appealing
Able to attract interest or draw favorable attention.

appeased
Satisfied; at peace with someone or something.

appeasing
Having an intention to pacify by acceding to demands or granting concessions.

applauded
Approved of and/or praised for something accomplished.

appraised
Considered in a comprehensive way; evaluated.

appreciate
To have gratitude toward a person, quality, or thing.

appreciated
1. Recognized with gratitude.
2. Fully understood or grasped.

appreciation
1. Thankful recognition for someone or something.
2. An understanding of the nature, meaning, quality, or magnitude of something.

appreciative
1. Having gratitude for someone or something.
2. Showing a favorable critical judgment or opinion.

apprehension
Fearful expectation or anticipation.

apprehensive
Fearful that something might happen.

approachable
Easy to meet, converse, or do business with.

appropriate
Suitable for a particular person, place, condition, etc.

approval
Acceptance and satisfaction for something or someone.

approved
Agreed upon by someone, such as an authority.

arbitrary
1. Impulsive in making decisions.
2. Subject to individual discretion or preference.

archaic
Extremely old or old-fashioned.

ardent
Feeling strong enthusiasm.

ardor
Intense love.

arduous
Requiring strenuous effort; difficult and tiring.

argumentative
Opposed to others' views.

aristocratic
1. Characteristic of nobility or the aristocracy.
2. Grand and stylish.

armored
Protected and safe.

aroused
1. Sexually stimulated.
2. Awakened, stimulated to action.

arrogant
Feeling unwarranted importance or overbearing pride.

artful
Marked by skill in achieving a desired end, especially with cunning or craft.

artfulness
Adroitness in taking unfair advantage.

articulate
Clear and fluent in communication.

artificial
Contrived by art rather than nature.

artistic
Naturally, creatively skilled.

artless
1. Lacking art or knowledge.
2. Simple and natural.

artsy
Strongly affected by the arts.

ascetic
Rigorously self-disciplined.

ashamed
Feeling shame, guilt, embarrassment, and/or remorse due to one's actions, characteristics, or associations.

asinine
Extremely silly or stupid.

asleep
1. In a state of unconsciousness.
2. Feeling a lack of sensation.

asocial
Hostile to or disruptive of normal standards of social behavior.

asperity
Harshness toward someone or something.

asphyxiated
Smothered by something.

aspiring
Desiring or striving for recognition or advancement.

assaulted
Attacked by someone or something.

assertive
Boldly self-assured without being aggressive; confident.

assessed
Judged or evaluated for something.

assiduous
Marked by care and persistent effort.

assuaged
Mitigated or relieved intensity from something.

assurance
Freedom from doubt; belief in oneself and one's abilities.

assured
Confident, secure, and certain.

astonished
Overwhelmingly surprised or shocked.

astonishing
1. Surprisingly great.
2. Stunning or overwhelming.

astounded
Affected with wonder.

astounding
Surprisingly great.

astute
Practical, hardheaded, and intelligent.

asymmetrical
Lacking symmetry; deformed or disproportionate.

atrabilious
Irritable as if suffering from indigestion.

atrocious
Exceptionally bad or displeasing.

atrophied
Diminished in size or strength.

atrophy
To gradually decline in effectiveness.

attached
1. Fond of and affectionate to a person, thing, or quality.
2. Joined in close association.

attachment
1. Affection for a person or an institution.
2. A connection with something.

attacked
Aggressive behavior or assault by someone or something.

attentive
Paying close and thoughtful attention to someone or something.

attentiveness
Consideration and thoughtfulness of others.

attracted
Drawn to a person, interest, place, or thing.

attraction
The quality of arousing interest, pleasure, or liking for someone or something.

attractive
1. Having power to arouse interest.
2. Pleasing to the senses.

atypical
Somewhat odd, strange, or abnormal; not representative of a group, class, or type.

audacious
Invulnerable to fear or intimidation.

austere
Stern and strict; forbidding in aspect.

austerity
Great self-denial; sternness.

authentic
Genuine, factual, and real.

authoritarian
Tyrannical; oppressive and controlling.

authoritative
Having authority, ascendancy, or influence.

autocratic
1. Offensively self-assured.
2. Absolutely powerful; domineering.

automated
Automatically processed.

automatic
Having inherent power of action or motion without conscious control.

available
Obtainable or accessible and ready; free to do something.

avarice
Extreme greed for material wealth.

avaricious
Immoderately desirous of acquiring something, such as wealth.

avenged
Having accomplished vengeance.

average
Lacking special distinction, rank, or status; ordinary.

averse
Strongly opposed to something.

aversion
Intense dislike of something or someone.

avid
Characterized by excessive desire or active interest and enthusiasm for something.

avoidance
Desire for prevention of something happening.

avoided
Shunned or kept clear of by someone or something.

awake
Completely conscious; not asleep.

awakened
Aroused or activated.

aware
Alert and fully informed.

awe
Profound respect or overwhelming wonder, surprise, and/or fear caused by someone or something.

awed
Feeling wonderment or reverence with (or without) fear.

awesome
Very good or great.

awestruck
Filled with reverential respect mixed with fear or wonder.

awful
Exceptionally bad or displeasing.

awkward
1. Uneasy or unsure and constrained.
2. Lacking grace or elegance.

awry
Off course or expectation.

babied

Cared for as a baby.

babyish

Like a baby.

backward

1. In the reverse of normal.
2. Relating to or characteristic of a past time.

bad

1. Wicked or immoral.
2. Undesirable or negative.
3. Sick and/or unwell.

badgered
Persistently irritated or annoyed by something or someone.

bad-tempered
Characterized by persistent anger.

baffled
Frustrated and perplexed.

baited
Lured, enticed, or entrapped.

balance
A state of equilibrium.

balanced
In equilibrium, in harmony with something, or in appropriate proportion.

baleful
Hostile and threatening and/or feeling a desire to cause harm.

bamboozled
Fooled or cheated.

banal
Boring and common in a predictable way.

banished
Expelled and forbidden to return from somewhere or something.

bankrupt
Completely depleted; financially ruined.

banned
Forbidden or prohibited; not allowed to participate or to be included in something.

bantered
Playfully teased in a light, humorous way.

bare
Naked or raw; exposed.

barracked
Heckled or jeered; shouted at in a disconcerting way.

barraged
Addressed continuously and persistently.

barred
Kept out; prevented from being included.

barren
Completely wanting or lacking.

base
Immoral; not adhering to ethical or moral principles.

bashful
Shy or self-consciously timid; disposed to avoid notice.

bathetic
Insincerely emotional.

battered
Repeatedly injured; beaten continuously.

batty
Mentally irregular; crazy.

bearable
Capable of being tolerated though unpleasant.

bearish
1. Pessimistic about something, such as the economy.
2. Grumpy and rude.

beastly
Very unpleasant; lacking human sensibility.

beat
Very tired or defeated.

beaten
1. Physically or mentally attacked.
2. Completely overcome by someone or something; defeated.

beatific
Blissfully joyful.

beautiful
Delighting the senses or exciting admiration.

beckoned
Invited; encouraged to join or follow.

bedazzled
Greatly impressed to the point of amazement or confusion.

bedeviled
Tormented or harassed.

bedraggled
Soiled and unkempt.

befriended
Invited to friendship with another.

befuddled
Confused or perplexed; unable to think clearly.

beggarly
Poor as would befit a beggar.

begged
Receiving an earnest request from someone or something; entreated.

begrudging
1. Envious or covetous of something.
2. Reluctant or giving in to something half unwillingly.

beguiled
Charmed or enchanted, typically in a misleading or deceptive way.

behind
Lower in rank, status, or quality; inferior.

beholden
Morally obligated.

beleaguered
Persistently annoyed.

believed in
Feeling as if someone has confidence, trust, and faith in you.

believing
Confident about something.

belittled
Made to seem smaller, less (especially in worth), or unimportant, based on the actions and/or comments of another.

belittling
Disparaging toward someone.

bellicose
Aggressive and ready to fight.

belligerence
A hostile or warlike attitude or nature.

belligerent
Hostile and aggressive.

belonging
Happiness from a secure relationship.

beloved
Dearly loved.

bemused
Perplexed by many conflicting situations or statements.

bemusement
Confusion resulting from failure to understand.

benevolence
Kindness from someone or something.

benevolent
Kind to someone or something.

benign
Kind and gentle.

bent
Fixed in purpose.

benumbed
1. Numb or insensitive.
2. Feeling an absence of sensation.

berated
Scolded severely or angrily.

bereaved
Sorrowful from loss or deprivation.

bereft
Unhappy in love; suffering from unrequited love.

berserk
Wildly frenzied and out of control.

beseeched
Receiving an earnest request.

beseeching
Urgently appealing; imploring.

besieged
Distressed or worried.

besmirched
Charged falsely or with malicious intent.

besotted
1. Strongly infatuated.
2. Very drunk.

bestial
Lacking human sensibility.

betrayal
Violation of confidence; disloyalty.

betrayed
Exposed by broken trust or disloyalty.

better
Superior or improved in quality, condition, or effect.

bewildered
Perplexed and confused.

bewitched
Captured, as if under a magic spell.

bewitching
Captivating, as if casting a spell.

bias
Partiality that prevents objective consideration of an issue or situation.

biased
Favoring one person or side over another.

big
1. Large or overweight.
2. Significant in meaning.

bile
Anger and irritation.

bilious
Irritable, as if suffering from indigestion.

biting
Harsh or cruel.

bitter
Angry, hurt, and strongly resentful or cynical.

bitterness
Deep anger and ill will.

bizarre
Conspicuously or grossly unconventional or unusual.

black
Angry, resentful, or hostile.

blacklisted
Banished or boycotted.

blackmailed
Threatened or forced to do something.

blah
Bored and/or depressed.

blame
Responsibility for a lapse or misdeed.

blamed
Accused of being responsible for some lapse or misdeed.

blameless
Free of guilt; not subject to blame.

bland
Lacking stimulation; uninteresting.

blank
Lacking comprehension.

blanketed
Covered by something, as if with a blanket.

blasé
Nonchalantly unconcerned.

blasphemous
Grossly irreverent toward what is held to be sacred.

blasphemy
Disrespect for God or for something sacred.

blasted
Criticized harshly or violently.

bleak
Having little or no hope.

bled
Diffused or slowly drained of resources.

blessed
Highly favored or fortunate (as though by divine grace).

blessedness
Supreme happiness from good fortune.

blighted
Prevented from growing; spoiled or ruined by someone or something.

blind
Unable or unwilling to perceive or understand.

bliss
Extreme happiness.

blissful
Completely happy and contented.

blithe
Carefree, happy, and lighthearted.

blocked
1. Unable to remember or process.
2. Obstructed, closed off from an expected experience.

bloomed
1. Having reached full potential.
2. Beautiful and radiant.

blossomed
Developed or at a promising stage.

blossoming
Developing into one's full potential.

blown away
Extremely impressed.

bludgeoned
Overcome or coerced, as if by use of a heavy club.

blue
Sad or depressed.

blunt
Direct; without subtlety or evasion.

blurred
Unclear; distorted.

blurry
Uncertain; confused.

blustery
Noisily domineering.

boastful
Exhibiting self-importance.

bodacious
Impressive, excellent, and/or attractive.

boggled
Startled with amazement or fear.

bogus
Fraudulent; having a misleading appearance.

boiling
Agitated or extremely angry.

boisterous
Rowdy; noisy and lacking in restraint or discipline.

bold
Fearless, daring, confident, and courageous.

bombarded
Experiencing something continuous or persistent
(usually negative, such as questions from an angry
audience).

bombastic
Ostentatiously lofty in style.

bonkers
Mentally irregular; crazy.

bored
Weary from lack of interest.

boredom
Weariness from a lack of interest induced by something tedious.

boring
So lacking in interest as to cause mental weariness.

bossy
Offensively self-assured or given to exercising usually unwarranted power.

bothered
Troubled or inconvenienced and/or agitated by disruption.

bothersome
Irritating or annoying to someone or something.

bought
Paid for by favors or influence.

bouncy
Joyously enthusiastic; confident and lively.

bound
Confined by bonds.

braced
Ready for confrontation, danger, or something unpleasant or difficult.

brainwashed
Subjected to intensive forced indoctrination, resulting in the rejection of old beliefs and acceptance of new ones.

brainy
Unusually and impressively intelligent.

brash
Offensively bold.

bratty
Impolitely unruly (typically, of an ill-mannered child).

brave
Courageous; able to deal with danger or fear.

bravery
A quality of spirit that enables one to face danger or pain without fear.

brazen
Bold and shameless; defiant.

breathless
Short of breath from excitement.

breathtaking
Extremely beautiful or astonishing or awe-inspiring.

breezy
Fresh and animated.

bright
Smart and able to learn quickly.

bright eyed
Alert and lively.

bright eyed and bushy tailed
Feeling alert, eager, and full of energy.

brilliance
Unusual mental ability.

brilliant
Unusually and impressively intelligent.

brisk
Quick and energetic.

briskness
Liveliness and eagerness.

bristling
Offended or angry.

brittle
Lacking warmth and generosity of spirit.

broken
1. Tamed or trained to obey.
2. Weakened and made infirm.

brokenhearted
Full of sorrow.

brooding
Deeply and seriously thoughtful, contemplative.

broody
Deeply or seriously thoughtful.

browbeaten
Discouraged or frightened by threats or by a domineering manner; intimidated.

bruised
In emotional pain from a negative or bad experience.

brushed off
Barred from attention or consideration.

brutal
Disposed to inflict pain or suffering; punishingly harsh.

brutalized
Exposed to violence.

bubbly
Full of high spirits.

bugged
Annoyed or irritated by someone or something.

buggered
Very tired; exhausted.

bullheaded
Determined without thought or consideration.

bullied
Intimidated by force that induces fear and discouragement.

bullish
Optimistic about someone or something.

bummed
Disappointed about something.

bummed out
Sad or depressed about something.

buoyant
Lively and lighthearted; cheerful.

burdened
Restricted by responsibility.

burdensome
Taxing on someone or something; demanding.

buried
Overwhelmed with something.

burned out
Overworked or overwhelmed with stress.

bushed
Very tired or fatigued.

busted
Caught in the act of doing something wrong.

busy
Active or fully engaged or occupied.

buzzed
Lightly intoxicated.

bypassed
Avoided or ignored by someone or something.

caged
Trapped; confined in a cage.

cagey
Self-interested and shrewd in dealing with others.

cajoled
Persuasively flattered.

calculating
Acting with a specific goal.

callous
Insensitive and cruel toward others.

callousness
A lack of passion or feeling; hardheartedness.

callow
Young and inexperienced.

calm
Steady and without agitation; tranquil.

calmed down
Quiet or calm, especially after a state of agitation.

calmness
1. Steadiness of mind under stress.
2. An absence of agitation or excitement.

camaraderie
Mutual trust and friendship.

canny
Shrewd and having good judgment.

cantankerous
Unwilling to cooperate.

capability
An aptitude that may be developed.

capable
Qualified to do things well.

capricious
Characterized by sudden and unaccountable changes of mood.

captious
Prone to petty objections.

captivated
Strongly interested in someone or something.

captivating
Attractive and engaging; charming.

captivation
Great liking for something wonderful and unusual.

captive
1. Held in the grip of a strong emotion or passion.
2. Confined by someone or something.

captured
Confined or controlled by force.

care
Concern or interest in someone or something.

carefree
Free of trouble, worry, and care; cheerfully irresponsible.

careful
Cautiously attentive.

careless
Lacking attention, consideration, forethought, or thoroughness; not careful.

carelessness
The quality of not being careful or taking pains; negligence.

caring
Having empathy for others.

castigated
Severely punished.

casual
Informal; without plan, effort, or strain.

catatonic
In a mental stupor; unresponsive.

categorized
Placed into or assigned to a category.

catty
Marked by or arising from malice.

caught
Seized, delayed, or held up.

cautious
Careful or guarded.

cavalier
Gallant or courtly.

censored
1. Suppressed by someone or something.
2. Supervised or watched for a specific reason, such as for moral or lawful purposes.

censorious
Harshly critical.

censure
Harsh criticism or disapproval.

censured
Formally rebuked.

centered
1. Stable and calm.
2. Mentally balanced.

certain
Confident about something.

certainty
Trust in something.

chafed
Extremely irritated or angered.

chagrin
Distress due to the failure of something.

chagrined
Humiliated, ashamed, self-conscious, or ill at ease.

chained
Bound to something or someone.

challenged
Tested or disputed.

challenging
Difficult to communicate or work with.

changeable
Adaptable; capable of being changed.

changed
Transformed into something different.

chaotic
Completely unordered, unpredictable, and confusing.

charged
Fraught with great emotion.

charismatic
Characterized by an extraordinary ability to attract.

charitable
Full of love and generosity.

charity
Kindly and lenient attitude toward people.

charm
Attractiveness that interests, pleases, or stimulates.

charmed
Strongly attracted; filled with wonder and delight.

charming
Pleasing or delighting.

chary
Greatly cautious and wary.

chaste
Morally pure.

chastened
Disciplined or punished.

chastised
Severely censured.

chatty
Full of trivial conversation.

cheap
1. Embarrassingly stingy.
2. Tastelessly showy.

cheapened
Reduced in worth.

cheated
Deprived of something by deceit.

cheated on
Betrayed from infidelity of a significant other or lover.

cheeky
Offensively bold.

cheerful
Happy and optimistic.

cheerfulness
Spontaneous good spirits.

cheerless
Sad and gloomy.

cheery
Bright and pleasant.

cherish
To feel fondness and attachment to someone or something.

cherished
Fond affection for someone or something.

chic
Elegant and stylish.

chicken
1. Easily frightened.
2. Lacking confidence.

chided
Censured severely or angrily.

childish
Lacking maturity.

childless
Without offspring.

childlike
Characteristic of a child in simplicity and credulity.

chill
Calm and content.

chipper
Cheerful, lively, and self-confident.

chirpy
Lively and lighthearted.

chivalrous
Courteous and attentive to another.

choked
Constricted in a way that prevents something from flowing freely.

choleric
Easily moved to anger.

chosen
Selected by someone or something.

chuffed
Very pleased.

churlish
Rude and meanspirited.

circumspect
Heedful of potential consequences.

circumvented
Avoided or bypassed by someone or something.

civil
Adhering satisfactorily to social usages and sufficient (but not noteworthy) consideration for others.

civility
Formal or perfunctory politeness.

civilized
Refined in taste and manners.

clandestine
Secretive (sometimes to conceal illicit or deceptive purposes).

clarity
Free from obscurity and easy to understand.

classy
Elegant and fashionable.

claustrophobic
Abnormally afraid of a closed-in place or places.

clean
Free from impurities or restrictions or qualifications.

cleansed
Purged of an ideology, bad thoughts, or sins.

clear
Free from confusion or doubt.

clenched
Tightly closed.

clever
Quick and resourceful.

clingy
Having a desire to hold on to something or someone.

cloistered
Private or secluded.

close
Intimate in relevance or relationship to someone or something.

closed
Shut down or shut off to new ideas, actions, commitments, or relationships.

closed in
Blocked or enclosed by something.

closed-minded
Lacking readiness or willingness to receive new ideas.

closeness
Intimacy and a feeling of belonging together.

clouded
Apprehensive or unclear about something.

cloudy
Lacking clarity or certainty.

clownish
Buffoonish, zany, or playful.

clued in
Well informed.

clueless
Totally uninformed about what is going on.

clumsy
Lacking grace.

coarse
Lacking refinement, cultivation, or taste.

coaxed
Influenced or urged by gentle persuasion, caressing, or flattering.

cocksure
Excessively confident.

cocky
Overly self-confident.

coddled
Treated with excessive indulgence.

codependent
Controlled or manipulated by another.

coerced
Persuaded by force or threat.

cold
1. Sexually unresponsive.
2. Lacking compassion or warmth for someone or something.

collaborative
Compelled to work with others.

collapsed
Broken down from fatigue, illness, or sudden attack.

collected
Gathered, organized, or ready.

colorful
Expressive, interesting, lively, and/or creative.

comatose
In a state of deep and usually prolonged unconsciousness.

combative
Characterized by an inclination to dispute or disagree; ready to fight.

comfort
Relaxation, relief, or satisfaction.

comfortable
Free from stress; peace of mind.

comforted
Relieved and supported by someone or something.

comfy
Relaxed and comfortable.

commanding
Exercising authoritative control or power over something or someone.

committed
1. Bound or obligated, as under a pledge to a particular cause, action, or attitude.
2. Associated in an exclusive romantic relationship.

common
Not special in distinction or quality.

commonplace
Completely ordinary and unremarkable.

communicative
Able or tending to communicate.

companionable
Ready and able for companionship; friendly and sociable.

companionship
The sensation of being with someone.

comparative
Related to, based on, or involving comparison.

compared
Considered or described as similar, equal, or analogous.

compassion
A deep awareness of and sympathy for another's suffering.

compassionate
Sympathetic and concerned for others.

compatibility
1. Sympathetic understanding.
2. Capability of existing or performing in harmonious or congenial combination.

compatible
Able to exist and perform in harmonious or agreeable combination.

compelled
Forced to do something.

competent
Properly or sufficiently qualified, capable, or efficient.

competitive
Characterized by a fighting disposition.

competitiveness
An aggressive willingness to compete.

complacent
Content to a fault with oneself or one's actions.

complementary
Combined in such a way as to enhance or emphasize the qualities of each other or of another.

complete
Perfect and whole in every respect; having all necessary qualities.

complex
Difficult to analyze or understand.

compliant
Inclined to comply.

complicated
Difficult to analyze or understand.

complimentary
Having a desire to compliment.

complimented
Praised, respected, and/or esteemed.

composed
Free from agitation; calm and in control of oneself.

composure
Steadiness of mind under stress.

comprehension
An ability to understand the meaning or importance of something (or the knowledge acquired as a result).

compressed
The sensation of something squeezed or pressed together.

compromised
In danger, suspicion, or disrepute.

compromising
Mutually conceding or having a capacity to compromise.

compulsive
Feeling compelled to do certain things.

compunction
Deep regret or guilt (usually from some misdeed).

conceit
Excessive pride.

conceited
Having an exaggerated sense of self-importance.

concentrated
Focused on something.

concern
1. Sympathy for someone or something.
2. Anxiety or worry.

concerned
Deeply interested or worried about someone or something.

concupiscent
Characterized by vigorous passion or strong sexual desire.

condemnation
Strong disapproval.

condemned
Sentenced to punishment; punished.

condescending
Arrogant, patronizing to those considered inferior; acting superior.

confidence
Trust in oneself, in someone, or something.

confident
Having trust in oneself; self-assured.

confined
Deprived of freedom.

confirmed
1. Established or made firm.
2. Not subject to change.

conflict
Opposition or disagreement.

conflicted
Confused and having mutually inconsistent feelings.

conforming
Adhering or adapting to new or different conditions, established customs, or doctrines (especially in religion).

confounded
Confused and perplexed, usually caused by an unexpected experience or series of experiences.

confrontation
Discord resulting from a clash of ideas or opinions.

confrontational
Hostile or argumentative.

confronted
Accusing opposition and hostility from someone or something.

confused
Unable to think with clarity or act intelligently.

confusion
A lack of clear and orderly thought and behavior.

congenial
Compatible to someone or something.

congeniality
Compatibility between persons.

connected
Joined or linked together.

connection
A feeling of being connected to someone or something.

conned
Deprived of something by deceit.

conniving
Secretive in a pursuit of a fraudulent or illegal end.

conquered
Under control by force or authority.

conscientious
Extremely careful and taking great effort.

conscious
Aware of surroundings, sensations, and thoughts.

consecrated
1. Solemnly dedicated to a higher or sacred purpose.
2. Devoted to a deity or some religious ceremony or use.

conservative
Reluctant to accept changes and new ideas.

considerate
Concerned for the rights and feelings of others.

consideration
Kind and considerate regard for others.

considered
Taken into account.

consistency
A harmonious uniformity or agreement among things
or parts.

consistent
Reliable; capable of reproducing something.

consoled
Morally or emotionally supported by someone or
something; comforted.

consoling
Supportive and comforting.

conspicuous
Obvious to the eye or mind.

conspiring
Desiring to carry out some harmful or illegal act.

constant
1. Unvarying in nature.
2. Uninterrupted in time and indefinitely long; continuing.

consternated
Anxious from an unexpected experience.

constrained
Lacking spontaneity; not natural.

constraint
Thoughts or behavior controlled by someone or something.

constricted
Especially tense.

constructive
Useful in purpose.

consulted
Asked to provide advice or perspective (usually professionally).

consumed
Fully engaged.

contagious
Capable of transmitting something.

contained
Controlled or restrained.

contaminated
Made impure by something.

contemplation
A calm, lengthy, intent consideration.

contemplative
Deeply or seriously thoughtful.

contempt
Disrespect with intense dislike.

contemptible
Deserving of contempt or scorn.

contemptuous
Characterized by extreme contempt; scornful.

content
Satisfied; peacefully happy.

contented
Satisfied with things as they are.

contention
Strong disagreement.

contentious
Inclined to dispute or disagree.

contentment
Happiness with one's situation in life.

contradiction
Opposition between two conflicting forces or ideas.

contradictory
Mutually opposed or inconsistent; disagreeing.

contrary
Inclined to disagree or experience the opposite of what is expected.

contrite
Pained by guilt from an offense.

control
Power to direct or determine.

controlled
Restrained, managed, or kept within certain bounds.

controlling
Having and exerting influence and authority over someone or something.

convenience
The quality of something being useful and convenient.

convenient
Suited to one's comfort, purpose, or needs.

conventional
Unimaginative and conformist.

converted
Changed in nature, purpose, or function.

convicted
Guilty by proof or declaration from someone.

conviction
An unshakable belief in something without need for proof or evidence.

convinced
Persuaded; very sure.

convincing
Believable; truthful.

convivial
Feeling fondness and the joy of good company; festive.

cool
1. Unenthusiastic; calm and self-controlled, composed.
2. In style, popular, or great.

cooperative
Desiring and willing to work together with someone or something.

copacetic
Completely satisfied.

copied
Imitated by someone or something.

coping
Successful in doing, achieving, or producing (something) with the limited or inadequate means available.

coquettish
Playfully flirtatious.

cordial
Polite, friendly, and warm toward others.

cordiality
Warmth and friendliness.

cornered
1. Trapped with no apparent way out.
2. Forced to turn and face someone or something.

corralled
Feeling gathered; enclosed in a corral.

correct
1. Free from error; especially conforming to fact or truth.
2. Socially right.
3. In accord with accepted standards of usage or procedure.
4. Right in opinion or judgment.

corrosive
Spitefully sarcastic.

corrupt
Lacking integrity; dishonest, immoral, or evasive.

corrupted
Ruined in character or quality.

counter
Opposition to something.

counterfeit
Not genuine; imitating something superior.

courage
A quality of spirit that enables one to face danger or pain without showing fear.

courageous
Brave; unafraid of danger or pain.

courteous
Showing courtesy and gracious good manners.

courteousness
Gracious consideration toward others; good etiquette.

courtly
Refined or imposing in manner or appearance; befitting a royal court.

covert
Secret or hidden; not openly practiced, engaged in, shown, or avowed.

coveted
Greatly desired.

covetous
Painfully desirous of another's advantages.

cowardice
A lack of courage.

cowardly
Ignobly timid and fainthearted.

coy
Shy or modest in a playful or provocative way.

coziness
A state of warm, snug comfort.

cozy
Comfortingly warm and sheltered; feeling a warm or friendly and informal atmosphere.

crabby
Annoyed and irritable.

craftiness
Shrewdness as demonstrated by being skilled in deception.

crafty
Skilled in deception.

cramped
Constricted in size.

cranky
Easily irritated or annoyed.

crappy
Very bad, unwell, or unpleasant.

crass
So unrefined as to be lacking in discrimination and sensibility.

crave
To have a great desire for something.

craving
An intense desire for some particular thing.

crazed
Wildly insane.

craziness
Rashness and foolishness.

crazy
1. Intensely enthusiastic about someone or something.
2. Affected with madness or insanity.
3. Bizarre or fantastic.
4. Deranged and possibly dangerous.

creative
Having the ability or power to create.

credence
Confidence that something is true.

credulous
1. Lacking judgment or experience.
2. Gullible or open to belief.

credulousness
A tendency to believe too readily and therefore to be easily deceived.

creepiness
An uneasy sensation, as of insects creeping on one's skin.

creepy
Annoying and unpleasant.

crestfallen
Low in spirit; sad and disappointed.

criminal
Guilty of crime or serious offense; unlawful.

crippled
Deprived of strength or efficiency.

critical
1. Marked by a tendency to find and call attention to errors and flaws.
2. Very important.

criticized
Judged or censured.

cross
Annoyed and irritable.

crossed
Opposed by someone.

crotchety
Irritable and unsatisfied.

crowded
1. Overfilled or compacted or concentrated.
2. Disrupted or encroached on by someone.

crucified
Criticized harshly or violently.

cruddy
1. Characterized by obscenity.
2. Worthless or unwell.

crude
Conspicuously and tastelessly indecent.

cruel
Disposed to inflict pain or suffering; destitute of sympathetic kindness and pity.

cruelty
Extreme heartlessness.

crummy
Sick and/or uncomfortable.

crush
An intense attraction to or infatuation with someone.

crushed
Deeply disappointed.

cryptic
Puzzlingly terse.

cuckolded
Cheated on by one's partner in marriage.

cuckoo
1. Stupid and incompetent; foolish.
2. Crazy or insane.

cuddled
Receiving warm, comfortable affection from someone.

cuddly
Affectionate; inviting cuddling or hugging.

culled
Selected from a large group or rejected and removed.

culpable
Deserving of blame or censure as being wrong, evil, or injurious.

cultivated
Refined in taste and manners.

cultured
Refined in the arts, personal taste, behavior, and education.

cumbersome
1. Difficult to handle.
2. Disruptive to efficiency.

cunning
1. Attractive, especially by means of smallness, prettiness, or quaintness.
2. Skilled in deception.
3. Inventiveness and skill; ingeniousness.

cupidity
Extreme greed for material wealth.

curiosity
The sensation of wanting to learn more about something.

curious

Eager to investigate and learn or learn more.

curmudgeonly

Ill-tempered, surly, and forbidding.

cursed

1. Afflicted with something.
2. Addressed with profanity.

cushy

Without burden or demand.

cut

Separated or removed.

cute

1. Attractive, especially by means of smallness, prettiness, or quaintness.
2. Obviously contrived to charm.

cynical

1. Distrustful and/or doubtful of someone or something.
2. Concerned with one's own interests, with disregard to accepted standards of achieving them.

cynicism

Cynical distrust.

daffy
Silly or eccentric.

daft
Mentally irregular; feeling foolish or silly.

dainty
Delicately beautiful.

damaged
1. Harmed, injured, or spoiled.
2. Unjustly brought into disrepute.

damned
Condemned to eternal punishment.

dander
Anger and animosity.

danger
Condition of being susceptible to harm or injury.

dangerous
Threatening; causing fear or anxiety.

dared
Challenged to be courageous enough to try or to do something.

daring
Adventurously courageous; challenged to do something dangerous or foolhardy.

dark
1. Lacking enlightenment, knowledge, or culture.
2. Having evil characteristics or forces; wicked or dishonorable.

dashed
Having lost courage; dispirited.

dashing
1. Lively and spirited.
2. Up-to-date in dress and manners.

dastardly
Wicked and cruel; despicably cowardly.

daunted
Bothered to the point of discomposure.

dauntless
Invulnerable to fear or intimidation.

dazed
Stunned or confused and slow to react.

dazzled
1. Amazed by an experience.
2. Stupefied or dizzied by something overpowering.

dead
1. No longer having or seeming to no longer have life; expecting to not be alive.
2. Very tired.
3. Lacking human feeling or sensitivity; unresponsive.
4. Numb.

deadened
Devoid of sensation; insensitive.

deafened
Caused to hear poorly or not at all.

dear
Close or intimate in relation.

debased
Corrupt; ruined in character.

debated
Opposed through argument.

debauched
Unrestrained by morality.

debilitated
Weak; lacking energy or vitality.

debonair
1. Sophisticated and charming.
2. Cheerful, lively, and self-confident.

decadent
1. Luxuriously self-indulgent.
2. Excessively self-indulgent to the point of moral decay.

deceitful
Deliberately deceptive, especially by pretending one set of feelings and acting under the influence of another.

deceived
Feeling misled, cheated, or lied to.

decent
Socially or conventionally correct; refined or virtuous.

deception
A misleading falsehood.

deceptive
Misleading, either deliberately or inadvertently.

decided
Having made a decision about something.

decimated
Heavily damaged.

decisive
1. Having the power to determine an outcome.
2. Characterized by decision and firmness.

decrepit
1. Worn and broken down by hard use.
2. Lacking strength or vitality; feeble.

dedicated
Devoted to a cause, ideal, or purpose.

defamed
Charged for something falsely or with malicious intent; having one's good name and reputation attacked by someone.

defeat
Failure in attaining one's goals.

defeated
Demoralized and overcome by adversity; disappointingly unsuccessful.

defected
Failed or damaged; imperfect.

defective
Subnormal in intelligence or behavior.

defenseless
Lacking protection or support; without defense.

defensive
1. Having an attitude of protecting oneself.
2. Defending against or deterring aggression or attack.
3. Attempting to justify or defend in speech or writing.

deferent
Courteous in regard for people's feelings.

deferential
Respectful and considerate of someone or something.

defiant
Boldly resisting authority or an opposing force.

deficient
Inadequate in amount or degree.

defiled
Morally blemished; stained or impure.

definite
Precise; explicit and clearly defined; certain.

deflated
Brought low in spirit.

deformed
So badly formed or out of shape as to be ugly.

degenerate
Unrestrained by convention or morality.

degraded
Disrespected; inferior.

dehumanized
Divested of human qualities or attributes.

dejected
Low-spirited; downhearted.

delayed
1. Feeling not as far along as normal in development.
2. Feeling slowed down or put on hold.

delectable
1. Capable of arousing sexual desire.
2. Extremely pleasing to the sense of taste.

deleted
Removed or made invisible.

deleterious
Harmful to living things.

delicate
1. Exquisitely fine, subtle, and pleasing; susceptible to injury.
2. Easily hurt, broken, damaged, or destroyed.

delight
Extreme pleasure or satisfaction.

delighted
Greatly pleased.

delightful
Greatly pleasing or entertaining.

delinquent
Guilty of a misdeed.

delirious
Incoherent and restless; wildly excited or ecstatic.

demanding
Authoritative with high standards and/or expectations; forceful.

demeaned
1. Reduced in worth or character.
2. Suffering severe loss in dignity and respect.

demented
Affected with madness or insanity.

demolished
Ruined or destroyed.

demonized
Portrayed as wicked and threatening.

demoralized
Lacking hope; discouraged.

demoted
Lowered in rank or put in a less senior position.

demotivated
Lacking eagerness.

demure
Reserved or modest; playfully or provocatively shy.

denatured
Lacking natural qualities.

denial
A defense mechanism that denies painful thoughts.

denied
Refused of a request or desire.

denigrated
Unfairly criticized.

denounced
Publicly accused.

dense
Slow to learn or understand; lacking intellectual acuity.

dependable
Worthy of reliance or trust.

dependent
1. Held under the power or sovereignty of another or others.
2. Addicted to something or someone.

depleted
Suffering from complete loss of energy or resources.

deported
Expelled from a country.

depraved
Corrupted morally or by intemperance or sensuality.

deprecated
Deplored and/or belittled by someone.

depreciated
Reduced in value or self-worth.

depressed
Unhappy, typically with oneself or one's condition; suffering.

depression
1. A pessimistic sense of inadequacy and a despondent lack of activity.
2. Sadness and gloominess.

deprived
Severely lacking something considered important.

derailed
Obstructed or diverted from an intended path or course.

deranged
Driven insane.

desecrated
Treated with disrespect and contempt.

deserted
1. Left behind without assistance or support.
2. Remote from civilization.

deserving
Worthy of being treated in a particular way.

desiccated
Lacking vitality or spirit; lifeless.

desirable
Worthy of being chosen.

desire
A strong wish or want for something or someone.

desired
Wanted intensely.

desirous
Eagerly wishful.

desolate
Lonely, unhappy, or miserable.

despair
Helpless loss of hope.

despairing
Helpless and desperate.

desperate
1. Extreme urgency for a great need or desire.
2. Nearly hopeless.

despicable
Morally reprehensible.

despise
To have contempt or disdain for someone or
something.

despised
Treated with dislike or contempt.

despoiled
Robbed and destroyed by force and violence.

despondent
Without or almost without hope or courage.

destitute
Poor enough to need help from others.

destroyed
Emotionally or spiritually ruined.

destructive
Characterized by a desire to destroy or cause harm.

desultory
Lacking a definite plan, regularity, or purpose; jumping from one thing to another.

detached
Lacking emotional involvement.

detachment
Separation or avoidance of emotional involvement.

detained
1. Deprived of freedom; confined.
2. Slowed down or delayed.

deteriorated
Progressively worse than before.

determined
Strongly motivated to succeed.

detest
To intensely dislike.

detestable
Offensive to others.

detested
Intensely disliked by others.

detoxified
Free of poisonous substances or qualities.

devalued
Lowered in worth or importance.

devastated
Overwhelmed or overpowered by shock or grief.

deviant
Different from an accepted norm.

devilish
1. Cunning, ingenious, or wicked, typical of a devil.
2. Evil and cruel.

devious
Insincere or deceitful; evasive.

devoid
Completely wanting or lacking.

devoted
Feeling love for and loyalty to someone or something.

devotion
Ardent love.

devoured
Completely overtaken or destroyed by something.

devout
Deeply religious.

dexterous
Skillful in physical movements, especially of the hands.

dictatorial
Expecting unquestioning obedience.

different
Distinct or separate.

difficult
Hard to control or work with; not easy.

diffident
Modest or shy from a lack of self-confidence.

diffused
Spread out.

dignified
Formal and/or stately; worthy of respect.

diligent
Careful and perseverant in carrying out tasks.

dim
Slow to learn or understand.

diminished
Less important or valuable.

diminutive
Very small.

diplomatic
Tactful in dealing with sensitive matters or people.

dire
Fraught with extreme danger; nearly hopeless.

direct
Straightforward in language or action.

directionless
Without objective, structure, goal, or destination.

dirgeful
Deeply mournful.

dirtied
Morally soiled.

dirty
1. Vile; despicable.
2. Unethical or dishonest.

disabled
Restricted in mental or physical functioning.

disaffected
Hostile or indifferent where one was formerly loving, affectionate, or friendly.

disagreeable
1. Not to one's liking.
2. Unpleasant to interact with.

disappointed
Sad or displeased from the failure to achieve expectations.

disappointment
Sadness or displeasure due to the failure to fulfill one's hopes or expectations.

disapprobation
Strong disapproval.

disapproval
Dislike or objection of something.

disapproving
Disliking something or what someone is doing.

disbelief
Inability to accept something as true; a rejection of belief or lack of faith.

disbelieved
Unaccepted as being honest and/or truthful.

disbelieving
Refusing to accept something as true.

discardable
Easily removed or replaced; expendable.

discarded
Cast away.

discerning
Showing keen insight and good judgment.

disciplined
1. Able to obey the rules and apply self-control.
2. Trained by instruction or exercise.

discombobulated
Thrown into confusion.

discomfited
Characterized by a loss of composure.

discomfort
Mental pain or distress.

discomforting
Uneasy, anxious, or embarrassed.

discomposed
Agitated and/or upset from a disturbance.

disconcerted
Unexpectedly confused; unsettled.

disconnected
Lacking contact with something or someone.

disconsolate
Sad beyond comforting.

discontent
Dissatisfaction or restless longing.

discounted
Barred from attention or consideration.

discouraged
Lacking confidence or hope; disheartened.

discovery
The detection, learning, or experience of something new or for the first time.

discredited
1. Brought into disrepute.
2. Suffering from shame.

discreet
Prudent or modest and wisely self-restrained.

discriminating
Careful in judgment and discernment, especially in matters of taste.

disdain
A lack of respect accompanied by a feeling of intense dislike.

disdained
Rejected with contempt.

disdainful
Extreme contemptuous; lacking respect for someone or something.

disembodied
Free from a body, physical form, or reality.

disenchanted
Disappointed by someone or something previously respected or admired; disillusioned.

disenfranchised
Deprived of the rights of citizenship, especially the right to vote.

disengaged
Emotionally detached.

disentangled
Free from entanglement.

disesteem
Disrespect or low opinion.

disfavored
Put at a disadvantage.

disgraced
Suffering shame.

disgraceful
Offensive to moral sensibilities and injurious to reputation.

disgruntled
Angry or sulky with dissatisfaction.

disguised
Concealed with the intent of misleading.

disgust
Strong dislike.

disgusted
1. A strong distaste, nausea.
2. Profound disapproval.

disgusting
Highly offensive; arousing aversion or disgust.

disharmonious
Lacking harmony.

disheartened
Lacking determination or confidence.

disheveled
Extremely disorderly.

dishonest
Deceptive or fraudulent; disposed to cheat or defraud or deceive.

dishonorable
Lacking honor or integrity; deserving dishonor.

dishonored
Shamed or disgraced.

disillusioned
1. Free from a belief.
2. Disappointed from the loss of belief.

disinclined
Unwilling because of mild dislike or disapproval.

disingenuous
Insincere; falsely appearing to be frank.

disinterested
Unaffected by interest.

disjointed
Lacking order or connection.

dislike
Aversion or antipathy; distasting of or hostile toward someone or something.

disliked
Feeling aversion or hostility from someone.

dislocated
Out of place.

dislodged
Removed or forced out from a position.

disloyal
Lacking allegiance or support for someone or something.

dismal
Depressed; dejected.

dismayed
Struck with fear.

dismissed
Barred from attention or participation.

dismissive
Indifferent or disregarding.

disobedient
Unwilling to submit to authority.

disobeyed
One's demands, instructions, or wishes refused.

disorderly
Undisciplined and unruly.

disorganized
Lacking order or methodical arrangement or function.

disoriented
A loss of bearings; confused as to time or place or personal identity.

disowned
Cast off and unacknowledged.

dispassionate
Unaffected by strong emotion.

dispensable
Unimportant; easily removed.

dispirited
Lacking enthusiasm or hope; having low spirits.

displeased
Annoyed or unhappy with someone or something.

displeasure
Annoyance or dissatisfaction with someone or something.

disposable
Unimportant; expendable.

dispossessed
Spiritually homeless or deprived of security.

disputed
Disagreed with over something.

disquiet
Anxiety or worry.

disquieted
Anxiously uneasy.

disregard
Willful lack of caring and attention.

disregarded
Ignored or forgotten; accidentally not noticed.

disrelish
Dislike or distaste.

disrepute
Low esteem from loss of reputation.

disrespect
Lack of regard or courteous behavior.

disrespected
Receiving little or no respect.

disrespectful
Rude and discourteous.

disruptive
Responsible for disruption.

dissatisfied
Feeling unhappy with someone or something.

dissected
Taken apart and analyzed.

dissed
Disrespected; criticized.

dissident
Opposing official policy.

dissipated
Overindulged in sensual pleasures.

dissociated
Disconnected from someone or something.

dissolute
Unrestrained by morality.

distant
Lacking intimacy or far apart in relevance, relationship, or kinship.

distaste
Intense dislike; disagreeableness.

distasteful
Offensive to others.

distempered
Characterized by a predominance of a passion or appetite or deranged anger; ill-humored.

distorted
Mentally or morally twisted.

distracted
Unable to concentrate; preoccupied, anxious, and/or disturbed.

distractible
Easily distracted.

distraught
Deeply agitated.

distressed
Anxiously uneasy, troubled, or grieved.

distrust
Doubt about someone's honesty; suspicion or loss of faith in someone or something.

distrusted
Regarded as untrustworthy; regarded with suspicion.

distrustful
Lacking trust in someone or something.

disturbed
Agitated or troubled; unstable.

ditzy
Scatterbrained or silly.

diverted
Distracted or turned away.

divided
Separated into parts or pieces.

divorced
Formally or legally dissolved from being associated with someone or something.

dizzy
Feeling a whirling sensation; giddy or frivolous.

docile
1. Willing to be taught, led, supervised, or directed.
2. Gentle; submissive.

dogged
Stubbornly unyielding.

dogmatic
Certain of unproved or unprovable principles.

doldrums
A state of stagnation and/or depression.

doleful
Sorrowful; mournful.

dolorous
Greatly sorrowful or distressed.

domestic
Fond of or characteristic of home life and family.

domesticated
Accustomed to home life.

dominant
Influential or controlling of someone or something.

dominated
Controlled or ruled by a superior authority or power.

domineered
Controlled or ruled in a cruel and autocratic manner; tyrannized.

done
Having a sense of completion.

doom
An unpleasant or disastrous destiny.

doomed
Marked by bad fortune.

dopey
Slow and/or stupefied due to a lack of sleep or a drug.

dorky
Dull and stupid; unfashionable.

doubt
Uncertainty about something.

doubtful
Fraught with uncertainty or doubt.

doughty
Brave and persistent; resolute and without fear.

dour
Harshly uninviting; gloomy.

dowdy
Lacking smartness or taste.

down
Filled with melancholy and despondency.

downcast
Despondent and/or depressed.

downhearted
Discouraged; depressed.

downtrodden
Abused by people in power.

drained
Very tired.

dramatic
Sensational in appearance or thrilling in effect.

drastic
Forceful, extreme, and rigorous.

drawn
Feeling an attraction, desire, interest, or pull to approach something.

drawn in
Pulled inward.

dread
Fearful expectation or anticipation.

dreadful
Intensely unpleasant.

dreamy
Relaxed and happy; filled with wonder.

dreary
Lifeless and dull; gloomy.

driven
Strongly motivated to succeed.

droopy
Lacking strength or spirit.

dropped
In a state of exhaustion or death.

drubbed
Beaten thoroughly and conclusively in a competition or fight.

drunk
1. Intoxicated from something, such as alcohol.
2. Feeling an emotion so intensely as to be entirely dominated by it.

dry
1. Humorously sarcastic or mocking.
2. Lacking interest or stimulation; dull and lifeless.

dubious
Uncertain or doubtful.

dull
Lacking liveliness or animation; bored or boring.

dulled
Caused to lose or having lost interest because of overexposure.

dumb
Slow to learn or understand; lacking intellectual acuity.

dumbfounded
As if struck dumb with astonishment and surprise.

dumped
Rejection from severed ties, usually unceremoniously or irresponsibly.

duped
Fooled; deceived.

dutiful
Willingly obedient out of a sense of duty and respect.

dwarfed
Small by comparison.

dynamic
Characterized by action, forcefulness, or force of personality.

dysfunctional
Impaired in function.

dysphoric
Unwell or unhappy from distress.

eager
Characterized by intense desire or impatient expectancy.

eagerness
Enthusiasm to do or to have something.

early
At or near the beginning of a period of time or course of events; before the usual or expected time.

earnest
Characterized by sincere and intense conviction; serious.

earthy
Not far removed from or suggestive of nature.

ease
Free from effort; relaxed and gentle.

eased
Lessened intensity of something.

easy
Not difficult; requiring little effort.

easygoing
Relaxed and informal.

ebullient
Joyously unrestrained.

eccentric
Conspicuously or grossly unconventional or unusual.

eclectic
Characterized by an influence of ideas, style, or taste from a broad and diverse range of sources.

eclipsed
Overshadowed by someone or something.

economical
Careful to not waste resources.

ecstatic
Greatly enraptured or delighted.

edgy
1. Tense and/or nervous.
2. Fashionably risky or innovative.

edified
Instructed and encouraged in moral, intellectual, and spiritual improvement.

educated
Fully informed of the problem involved.

effaced
Insignificant or inconspicuous.

effective
Producing or having the capacity to produce an intended result or having a striking effect.

effeminate
Feminine; unmanly.

effervescent
Excited and enthusiastic.

effete
Deprived of vigor and the ability to be effective.

efficacious
Having the power to produce an intended effect.

efficient
Effective without wasting time, effort, or expense.

effusive
Showing heartfelt gratitude.

egocentric
Self-centered; with little regard for others.

egotistical
Having false pride, an exaggerated sense of self-importance.

elastic
Able to adjust readily to different conditions.

elated
Exultantly proud and joyful.

elation
Pride, joy, and optimism.

elderly
Advanced in years; old in age.

electric
1. Affected by emotion, as if by electricity; thrilling.
2. Exceptionally tense.

electrified
Suddenly and intensely excited.

elegant
Refined and tasteful in appearance, behavior, or style.

elegiac
Sorrowful (often for something past).

elevated
High in moral or intellectual value; increased in nature or style.

eloquent
Communicating readily, clearly, or effectively.

elusive
Difficult to detect or grasp by the mind or analyze.

emancipated
Free from traditional social restraints.

emasculated
Deprived of strength or vigor.

embarrassed
Uncomfortable due to shame or wounded pride;
self-conscious.

embarrassment
Self-consciousness, shame, or awkwardness.

embittered
Bitter or resentful.

emotional
Determined or actuated by emotion rather than
reason.

emotionless
Unmoved by feeling; indifferent.

emotive
Inclined to expressing emotion.

empathetic
Sensitive to another's feelings and/or experience.

empathic
Comprehensive of others' states.

empathy
A feeling of understanding and ability to enter into another's feelings.

emphatic
Forceful and definite.

empowered
Strong, confident, and/or with authority.

empty
Void of emotion.

emulation
Ambition to equal or excel.

emulous
Eager to surpass others.

enabled
Rendered capable or able to accomplish some task.

enamored
Unreasonably fond of or in love with someone or something.

enchanted
Influenced with delight; charmed.

enclosed
Closed in, surrounded, or included within.

encouraged
Inspired with confidence.

encouraging
Supportive and inspiring.

encumbered
Loaded to excess or impeded by a heavy load.

endangered
Put in a dangerous, disadvantageous, or difficult position; threatened.

endearing
Lovable, especially in a childlike or naive way.

endowed
Provided or supplied or equipped with (especially by inheritance or nature).

endurance
Power to withstand hardship or stress.

energetic
Healthy in capacity for vigorous activity.

energized
Motivated and full of energy.

energy
Strength and vitality.

enervated
Mentally or morally weakened; drained of energy.

engaged
Busy, fully occupied.

engaging
Attractive and interesting.

engrossed
Completely engaged in something.

engulfed
Fully devoted.

enhanced
Increased or intensified in value, beauty, or quality.

enigmatic
Not easy to understand; mysterious.

enjoyment
Pleasure from something.

enlightened
Having a rational, modern, and well-informed outlook.

enlivened
Cheerful and sprightly.

enmeshed
Entangled or caught, as if in a mesh.

enmity
Actively opposed or hostile.

ennobled
Noble and dignified.

ennui
Boredom from something tedious.

enraged
Violently angry.

enraptured
Intensely pleased; ecstatic.

enriched
Improved in quality.

enslaved
Lacking freedom or choice.

entangled
Deeply involved, especially in something complicated.

enterprising
Imaginative, initiating, and ready to undertake new projects.

entertained
Pleasantly occupied.

enthralled
Filled with wonder and delight.

enthrallment
A great liking for something wonderful and unusual.

enthused
Excited for or about something.

enthusiastic
Greatly excited and interested.

enticed
Tempted or lured by promise and/or pleasure.

enticing
Highly attractive and able to arouse hope or desire.

entitled
Qualified for or deserving of something by legal, awarded, granted, inherited, or perceived right.

entombed
Placed in a tomb.

entranced
Filled with wonder and delight, with one's entire attention focused on someone or something.

entrapped
Caught, as if in a trap.

entrenched
Established firmly and securely.

entrepreneurial
Willing to take risks in order to make a profit.

entrusted
Trusted by someone or something.

envenomed
Bitter or resentful.

envied
Admired with jealousy.

envious
Painfully desirous of another's advantages.

envy
Jealous admiration.

equal
The same in quantity, value, or measure as another.

equality
The quality of being the same.

equanimous
In full control of one's faculties.

equipped
Provided or fitted out with what is necessary, useful, or
appropriate.

equitable
Fair to all parties as dictated by reason and conscience.

eradicated
Destroyed completely, as if down to the roots.

erasable
Having the potential for elimination.

erased
Removed, as if rubbed out of existence.

eros
Desire for sexual intimacy.

erotic
Sexually arousing.

erratic
Unpredictable; quick to change.

essential
Feeling absolutely necessary; vitally important.

established
1. Valid beyond a reasonable doubt.
2. Grounded or firmly set in place.

esteem
Respect; delighted approval and liking.

esteemed
Respected; highly regarded.

estranged
Unloved; alienated.

ethereal
Characterized by unusual lightness and delicacy.

etiolated
Weak from stunted growth or development.

euphoria
Great (usually exaggerated) elation.

euphoric
Intensely excited and happy; elated.

evaded
Avoided by cunning or deceit.

evaluated
Critically judged or estimated by another.

evasive
Deliberately vague or ambiguous.

evil
Morally bad or wrong.

eviscerated
Removed, destroyed, or made meaningless.

exalted
Honored; extremely happy.

exanimate
Deprived of life; no longer living.

exasperated
Greatly annoyed; out of patience.

excellent
Very good.

exceptional
Far beyond what is usual in magnitude or degree.

excessive
Unrestrained; beyond normal limits.

excitable
Easily excited.

excited
Energetically and/or sexually aroused; stimulated.

excitement
Lively and cheerful joy.

excluded
Left out; not included.

excoriated
Censured or criticized severely.

exculpated
Freed from any question of guilt.

excused
Granted exemption.

execrated
Loathed and/or cursed by another.

exempt
Freed from or not subject to an obligation or liability
(e.g., taxes) to which others or other things are subject.

exhausted
Drained of energy or effectiveness; extremely tired.

exhilarated
Very happy; joyful.

exhilaration
Lively and cheerful joy.

exigent
Urgent and demanding attention.

exiled
Expelled from one's native country.

exonerated
Freed from any question of guilt; released from obligation.

exorcised
Expelled through adjuration or prayers.

exotic
Strikingly strange or unusual.

expansive
1. Exaggerated in euphoria and delusions of grandeur.
2. Open and willing to communicate.

expectant
Eagerly anticipative.

expectation
Anticipation with confidence of fulfillment.

experienced
Having knowledge or skill from observation or participation.

experimental
Innovative; willing to try something new.

exploitative
Desire and/or intention to use something or someone for personal advantage.

exploited
Taken advantage of.

explosive
Ready to suddenly burst out with emotion—anger, joy, etc.

exposed
Unprotected; vulnerable.

expressive
Effectively conveying feelings.

expunged
Completely removed from something; destroyed.

extraordinary
Beyond what is ordinary or usual; highly unusual, exceptional, or remarkable.

extravagant
1. Unrestrained in expression.
2. Recklessly wasteful.

extreme
In the greatest possible degree, extent, or intensity.

extricated
Released from entanglement of difficulty.

extroverted
At ease in talking to others.

exuberant
Joyously unrestrained.

exultant
Joyful and proud, especially because of triumph or success.

exultation
Extreme joy.

fabulous
Extremely pleased.

facetious
Flippant with deliberate, inappropriate humor.

factious
Disagreeing with another opinion; dissenting
(especially dissenting with the majority opinion).

failure
A lack of success.

faint
Weak in conviction, boldness, or courage.

fainthearted
Lacking conviction, boldness, or courage.

fair
Free from favoritism, self-interest, bias, or deception; conforming with established standards or rules.

faith
Complete trust and/or confidence in someone or something.

faithful
1. Steadfast in affection or allegiance.
2. Not having sexual relations with anyone except one's husband or wife or one's boyfriend or girlfriend.

fake
Fraudulent; having a misleading appearance.

fallen
Subjected to sin or depravity.

fallible
Likely to fail or make errors.

fallow
Undeveloped but potentially useful.

false
Deliberately deceptive.

faltering
Unsteady in speech or action.

familiar
1. Common and ordinary; not strange.
2. Well-informed or knowing thoroughly about something.
3. Well-known or easily recognized.

famished
Extremely hungry.

famous
Widely known and esteemed.

fanatical
Excessively enthusiastic for and devoted to a cause or idea.

fanciful
Imaginative and unrealistic.

fancy
A desire or liking for someone or something.

fantabulous
Very good; of the highest quality.

fantastic
Extraordinarily good or great.

farcical
Broadly or extravagantly humorous; resembling farce.

fascinated
Curious and interested.

fascinating
Capable of arousing and holding attention.

fascination
Great liking for something wonderful and unusual.

fashed
Troubled or worried.

fashionable
Elegant, tasteful, or refined in manners or dress.

fast
1. Capable of acting or moving quickly.
2. Unwavering in devotion to a friend, vow, or cause.

fastidious
Hard to please; excessively concerned with cleanliness.

fatalistic
Submitting to fate or an inevitable predetermination.

fatherless
Not having a known or legally responsible father.

fatherly
Paternal, kind, and protective.

fatigued
Drained of energy or effectiveness; extremely tired; completely exhausted.

fatuous
Extremely silly or stupid.

favor
Approval for someone or something.

favored
Preferred above all others and treated with partiality.

fazed
Lacking composure; disturbed.

fear
Afraid, anxious, or apprehensive about a possible or probable situation or event.

feared
Regarded with fear by others.

fearful
Lacking courage; fainthearted, dreadful, or terrorized.

fearless
Oblivious of dangers or perils or calmly resolute in facing them.

feckless
Unfit to assume responsibility.

fed up
Having a strong distaste for a situation; upset.

feeble
Pathetically lacking in force or effectiveness.

feel
To have a sensation or intuitive awareness; to experience.

feeling
Experiencing affective and emotional states.

feisty
1. Spunky in courage.
2. Feeling quick to take offense.

felicitous
Pleased and fortunate.

feminine
Characteristic of a woman.

fermented
Agitated or excited.

ferocious
1. Savagely fierce.
2. Extremely and violently energetic.

fervent
Intensely emotional.

fervid
Excessively passionate.

fervor
Great warmth and intensity.

festive
Joyful and merry.

fettered
Bound by chains fastened around the ankles.

feverish
Intensely agitated or frenetic with excitement.

fickle
Erratically changeable in affections or attachments.

fidelity
Faithfulness to a person.

fidgety
Nervous and unable to relax.

fiendish
Extremely evil or cruel; expressive of cruelty or
befitting hell.

fierce
Extremely and violently energetic.

fiery
Very intense.

filthy
Disgustingly dirty; filled or smeared with offensive
matter.

fine
Satisfactory or in satisfactory condition.

finesse
Skilled delicacy.

finicky
Exacting, especially about details.

finished
Brought to an end; completed.

fired
Dismissed from a job.

firm
Strong and sure.

first
1. At the beginning of something.
2. Ranked above all others.

first class
The highest rank in a classification.

fit
Physically and mentally sound or healthy.

fixated
Attached to a person or thing in a neurotic way.

fixed
Securely placed, fastened, or set.

flabbergasted
Overcome with amazement; astonished.

flagellated
Whipped or beaten.

flaky
Conspicuously or grossly unconventional or unusual; eccentric.

flamboyant
Attractive through exuberance, confidence, and stylishness.

flappable
Excitable and quick to lose one's composure.

flared up
Showing sudden and intense emotion.

flat
Lacking stimulating characteristics; uninteresting.

flattered
Praised, often somewhat dishonestly.

flawed
Imperfect or defective.

fleeced
Ripped off; taken advantage of.

flexible
Capable of being changed.

flighty
1. Guided by whim and fancy.
2. Unpredictably excitable.

flimsy
Lacking substance or significance.

flip
Marked by casual disrespect; not serious.

flippant
Showing inappropriate levity.

flipped out
1. Excited, delighted, or surprised.
2. Mad or crazy.

flirtatious
A playful attempt to attract or be loved by someone or something without serious intention.

flirty
Amorous without serious intention; playful.

flogged
Seriously beaten.

floored
Surprised greatly.

fluid
1. Flowing; unconstrained.
2. Smoothly elegant or graceful.

flummoxed
Bewildered or perplexed.

flush
1. A rush of emotion.
2. An abundant supply of money or possessions of value.

flustered
Agitated and confused.

fluttery
Nervous or excited.

focused
Having concentrated attention or energy on something.

foggy
Stunned or confused and slow to react (from blows, drunkenness, or exhaustion).

foiled
Disappointingly unsuccessful because of the actions of someone or something.

followed
Pursued; feeling the persistent presence of someone or something following you.

fond
Warmly affectionate; having a strong preference or liking for someone or something.

fondness
A predisposition to like something.

foolhardy
Defiantly disregarding danger or consequences.

foolish
Devoid of good sense or judgment.

footloose
Free to go or do as one pleases.

forbearing
Showing patient and unruffled self-control and restraint under adversity; slow to retaliate or express resentment.

forbidden
Restricted from use or mention.

forced
Imposed by coercion or physical power.

forceful
Strong and powerful; vigorous and assertive.

foreboding
The feeling that something bad or evil will happen.

foreign
Unfamiliar or out of place; strange.

forgetful
Deficient in retentiveness or range; likely to not remember.

forgettable
Easily forgotten.

forgivable
Easily excused or forgiven.

forgiven
Pardoned; absolved.

forgotten
Left behind; unnoticed inadvertently.

forlorn
Hopeless; sad and abandoned or lonely.

formal
In accord with established forms and conventions and requirements.

formidable
Extremely impressive in strength or excellence.

forsaken
Deserted; abandoned.

fortified
Strengthened or invigorated by something.

fortitude
Strength of mind that enables one to endure adversity with courage.

fortunate
Having good fortune.

forward
Lacking restraint or modesty.

foul
Highly offensive; arousing aversion or disgust.

fouled
Treated unfairly, disgraced, or wronged in some way.

fractious
Stubbornly resistant to authority or control; unruly; irritable.

fractured
Broken into pieces.

fragile
Vulnerably delicate.

fragmented
Divided; having destroyed unity.

frail
Physically weak.

framed
Accused or guilty by use of false evidence.

frank
Direct in manner or speech; without subtlety or evasion.

frantic
Excessively agitated; distraught with fear.

fraternal
Befitting a brother.

fraudulent
Having the intention to deceive.

frazzled
Exhausted and worn out.

freaked
Having lost one's nerve.

freaked out
Having lost one's nerve.

freakish
Conspicuously or grossly unconventional or unusual.

freaky
Strange and somewhat frightening.

free
Not limited or hampered; not under compulsion or restraint.

frenetic
Excessively agitated; energetic and out of control.

frenzied
Out of control; distraught with fear.

fresh
1. Having restored energy.
2. Clean and new.

fretful
Nervous and unable to relax; distressed or irritated.

fried
Worn out; exhausted.

friendless
Excluded from society; alone.

friendly
Helpful and supportive; kind and pleasant.

friendship
Trust, support, and kindness shared with someone or something.

frightened
Thrown into intense fear or desperation.

frightful
1. Provoking horror.
2. Very unpleasant, serious, or shocked.

frigid
1. Devoid of warmth and cordiality; unfriendly.
2. Sexually unresponsive.

frisky
Playful like a lively kitten.

frivolous
Not serious or sensible: carefree.

frolicsome
Energized and playful.

frugal
1. Economically cautious; thrifty.
2. Avoiding waste; sparing.

fruitful
Productive or conducive to producing in abundance.

frustrated
Distressed and annoyed.

frustration
Annoyance at being hindered, criticized, or thwarted in attaining one's goals.

fuddled
Confused from drinking alcohol.

fulfilled
Satisfaction from accomplishment.

full
1. Filled to satisfaction.
2. At a peak or culminating point.

fuming
Mad, angry, or furious.

fun
Enjoyable or amusing.

functional
Fit or ready for use or service.

funereal
1. Suggestive of a grave or burial.
2. Mournful and somber.

funky
1. Stylish and modern in an unconventional way.
2. In a state of cowardly fright.

funny

1. Amusing and humorous.
2. Unusual in such a way as to arouse suspicion.

furious

Extremely and violently energetic.

fury

Intense anger.

fussy

1. Exacting, especially about details.
2. Annoyed and irritable.

gagged
Silenced by a type of gag.

gaiety
Festivity and merriment.

gain
An increase in something.

gallant
Especially attentive and respectful toward a woman; brave and/or heroic.

galled
Pained from rubbing the skin; irritated.

galvanized
Stimulated to action.

game
Willing to face danger; willing to participate.

garbled
Lacking orderly continuity.

garrulous
Full of trivial conversation.

gauche
Lacking social polish.

gaudy
Tastelessly showy.

gawky
Lacking grace in movement or posture.

gay
1. Bright and pleasant; cheerful.
2. Attracted to the same sex.

geeky
Deeply interested in, knowledgeable, and enthusiastic about a specific topic.

generous
Willing to give and share unstintingly.

genial
Warm and friendly; agreeable.

geniality
A disposition to be friendly and approachable (easy to talk to).

genius
Exceptional intellectual ability and originality.

gentle
Soft and mild; not harsh, stern, or severe.

genuine
Sincere and authentic; true.

giddy
Feeling a lack of seriousness; given to frivolity.

gifted
Feeling endowed with a talent or talents.

giggly
Prone to silly or nervous laughter.

giving
Kind and generous.

glad
Happy and appreciative.

gladness
Joy and pleasure.

gladsome
Full of gladness or joy.

glamorized
Glamorous and attractive.

glamorous
Having an air of allure, romance, and excitement.

glee
Great merriment.

gleeful
High-spirited with delight; joyful.

glib
Lacking intellectual depth.

gloomy
1. Filled with melancholy and despondency.
2. Depressingly dark; pessimistic.

glorious
Characterized by great beauty and splendor; grand.

glowing
1. Highly enthusiastic.
2. Radiantly beautiful.

glum
Dejected; morose.

gluttonous
Excessively greedy.

gnawing
Distressed; worried.

goaded
Compelled by force from someone or something.

goatish
Lusty and lecherous.

gobsmacked
Utterly astounded.

good
1. Agreeable or pleasing.
2. Morally excellent.
3. Having knowledge, skill, and aptitude.

good-hearted
Feeling kindness, sympathy, understanding, and generosity.

good-natured
Pleasant and kind.

goofy
Ludicrous, foolish.

gorgeous
Dazzlingly beautiful.

gothic
Gloomy and mysterious.

grabby
Desirous of acquiring something.

graceful
Beautiful in movement, style, form, or execution.

gracious
1. Courteous and/or polite.
2. Gentle and kind.

graded
Ranked or rated by someone or something.

grand
Extraordinarily good or great.

grandiose
Impressive because of unnecessary largeness or grandeur.

grasping
Understanding with difficulty.

grateful
Thankful for something.

gratefulness
Warm and friendly gratitude.

gratified
Happy and fulfilled; satisfied.

gratitude
Thankfulness and appreciation.

grave
Dignified and somber; serious.

gravity
Heaviness or seriousness from a situation.

great
1. Very good.
2. Having achieved distinction and honor.

greed
Excessive desire to acquire or possess more (especially more material wealth) than one needs or deserves.

greedy
Characterized by selfish desire for something.

green
1. Not fully developed or mature.
2. Naive and easily deceived or tricked.

gregarious
Outgoing; sociable.

grief
Intense sorrow caused by loss of a loved one (especially by death).

grim
Feeling uninviting; depressed.

groggy
Stunned or confused and slow to react.

groovy
Very good and/or very chic.

gross
1. Conspicuously and tastelessly indecent.
2. Unattractive or unwell.

grossed out
Having distaste for someone or something.

grotesque
1. Distorted and unnatural in shape or size; abnormal and hideous.
2. Ludicrously odd.

grouchy
Annoyed and irritable.

grounded
Calm and stable.

groveling
Showing submission or fear.

grown
Changed over time so as to be stronger, more nearly complete, or more useful.

grown-up
1. Fully developed
2. Adult.

grudging
Reluctant or unwilling to accept, admit, or give something.

grumpy
Annoyed and irritable.

guarded
Cautious and prudent.

guided
Led by something or someone.

guile
Shrewdness as demonstrated by being skilled in deception; crafty.

guilt
Remorse caused by feeling responsible for some offense.

guilt free
Having permission to enjoy without feeling unhappy for doing something wrong or bad.

guiltless
Free from evil or guilt; innocent.

guilty
Responsible for a reprehensible act.

gullible
Naive and easily deceived or tricked.

gumption
Fortitude and determination.

gushing
Showing unrestrained enthusiasm.

gushy
Extravagantly demonstrative.

gusto
Vigorous and enthusiastic joy.

gutless
Weak in willpower, courage, or vitality.

gutsy
Courageous and determined in the face of difficulties or danger; robust and uninhibited.

gutted
Completely empty.

haggard
Showing the effects of overwork, worry, or suffering.

haggled
Harassed from a dispute over terms or price of something.

halfhearted
Feeling little interest or enthusiasm.

hallowed
Greatly revered or respected.

hammered
1. Attacked or criticized forcefully and persistently.
2. Overwhelming defeat.
3. Very intoxicated.

hampered
Put at a disadvantage.

handicapped
Restricted in mental or physical functioning because of an accident, illness, or other condition.

handsome
Pleasing in appearance, especially by reason of conformity to ideals of form and proportion.

hanker
To have a strong and/or persistent desire.

hapless
Deserving of pity; unfortunate.

happy
Joyful and/or pleased.

happiness
A state of well-being, including emotions ranging from contentment to intense joy.

happy-go-lucky
Cheerful without worry about the future.

harangued
Critically and aggressively lectured.

harassed
Troubled persistently, especially with petty annoyances.

hardened
Made tough by habitual exposure.

hardheaded
Unreasonably rigid in the face of argument, entreaty, or attack.

hardhearted
Devoid of feeling for others.

hard-pressed
Feeling heavily burdened.

hardy
1. Invulnerable to fear or intimidation.
2. Having rugged physical strength; inured to fatigue or hardships.

harmed
Injured or adversely affected by something.

harmless
Lacking a desire or ability to cause harm.

harmonious
Agreeable, friendly, and pleasing; free from disagreement or dissent.

harnessed
Controlled and directed by someone or something.

harried
Troubled persistently, especially with petty annoyances.

harsh
1. Unpleasantly stern.
2. Sharply disagreeable; rigorous.

hassled
Annoyed continually or chronically.

haste
A condition of urgency making it necessary to hurry.

hasty
Excessively quick.

hate
Intense dislike; antipathy or aversion.

hated
Treated with dislike or contempt.

hateful
1. Contemptuous and filled with hate.
2. Having an intention or desire to do something evil.

hatred
Intense dislike.

haughty
Feeling arrogantly superior.

haunted
1. Excessively or compulsively concerned with something.
2. Afflicted or disquieted.

hazy
Confused; unclear.

headstrong
Stubborn and self-willed.

heady
1. Extremely excited, as if by intoxicant.
2. Characterized by good judgment or common sense in practical matters.
3. Defiant and disregarding danger or consequences.

healed
Freed from illness or injury.

healthy
1. Having good health in body or mind; free from infirmity or disease.
2. Financially secure and functioning well.
3. Having good judgment.

heard
Content that information communicated has been received.

heartache
Anguish or grief typically caused by the loss or absence of a loved one.

heartbroken
Full of sorrow.

heartened
Cheerful and confident.

heartfelt
Sincerely earnest.

heartiness
Active strength of body or mind.

heartless
Devoid of courage or enthusiasm.

heartsick
Despondent; without or almost without hope.

hearty
Friendly; without reservation.

heated
Intensely emotional.

heavenly
Very good; wonderful.

heavy
Having great psychological weight; weighted down, especially with sadness, troubles, or weariness.

heckled
Challenged aggressively by someone.

hectic
Chaotic and very busy with activity.

held
Restrained by someone or something.

helped
Improved from the assistance of someone or something.

helpful
Serving a useful function.

helpless
Deprived of strength; unable to function independently.

henpecked
Harassed by persistent nagging.

herded
Crowded together.

heroic
Extremely courageous, especially when actions are courageously undertaken in desperation or as a last resort.

hesitant
Indecisive; uncertain; slow to act.

hesitation
A certain degree of unwillingness.

hideous
1. Grossly offensive to decency or morality; causing horror.
2. So extremely ugly as to be terrifying.

high
A state of elation or ecstasy.

high-spirited
Joyously unrestrained.

hilarious
Responsible for and/or the cause of boisterous merriment or convulsive laughter.

hindered
Put at a disadvantage.

hoaxed
Subjected to a playful trick or joke.

hollow
Lacking substance or character.

homely
Lacking physical beauty or proportion.

homesick
Longing to return home.

honest
1. Indisposed to cheat or defraud; not deceptive or fraudulent.
2. Truthful to oneself and/or others.

honorable
Worthy of being honored; entitled to honor and respect.

honored
Highly respected.

hoodwinked
Influenced by slyness.

hope
A state of belief that some desire will be fulfilled.

hopeful
Optimistic; having an agreeable expectation.

hopeless
1. Despairing; without possibility of comfort or success.
2. Inadequate or incompetent.

hopelessness
Despair from abandoning hope of comfort or success.

hormonal
Feeling effects from hormones.

horny
In a state of great sexual desire.

horrendous
Extremely unpleasant.

horrible
Extremely unpleasant; terrible.

horrific
Causing horror.

horrified
Unpleasantly surprised; stricken with horror.

hospitable
Friendly, cordial, and generous.

hostile
Unfriendly and antagonistic; angry.

hostility
Deep-seated ill will from someone or something.

hot
1. Sexually stimulated.
2. Very angry.
3. Extremely eager or enthusiastic.

hotheaded
Quickly aroused to anger.

hot-tempered
Easily angered.

hounded
Pursued or chased relentlessly.

hubris
Overbearing pride or presumption.

huff
A state of irritation or annoyance.

huffy
Annoyed or irritated; quick to take offense.

huge
Unusually great in size.

humane
1. Kind and compassionate; benevolent.
2. Motivated by concern with the alleviation of suffering.

humble
Modest or meek; unpretentious.

humbled
Subdued or brought low in condition or status.

humiliated
Uncomfortable because of shame or wounded pride.

humility
A disposition to be humble; a lack of false pride.

humored
Amused; put in a good mood.

humorous
Full of humor; funny and amusing.

hunger
A strong desire.

hungover
Suffering from a hangover after drinking alcohol.

hungry
Feeling a need or desire to eat food.

hunted
Pursued or chased relentlessly.

hurried
Rushed; pressed to move fast.

hurt
Psychologically or emotionally suffering.

hustled
Forced or coerced into something aggressively and/or hurriedly.

hyper
Unusually energetic.

hyperactive

More active than normal.

hypervigilant

Intensely aware.

hypnotic

Attracting and holding interest, as if by a spell.

hypnotized

Having one's attention fixated, as though by a spell.

hypocritical

Having double standards or applying a standard to others that is not applied to oneself.

hysteria

1. Violent mental agitation.
2. Excessive or uncontrollable fear.

hysterical

Excessively or uncontrollably emotional.

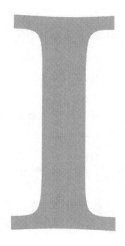

icky
Very bad.

idealistic
High in moral or intellectual value; elevated in nature or style.

idiosyncratic
Uniquely peculiar to someone; eccentric.

idiotic
Insanely irresponsible and/or stupid or unintelligent.

idle
1. Not active.
2. Lazy or slothful.

idolize
To revere and love and/or deeply admire someone or something.

idolized
Regarded with deep or rapturous love (especially as if for a god).

ignoble
Lacking nobility in character or quality or purpose.

ignominious
Deserving of disgrace or shame; discreditable.

ignominy
Shame; disgrace.

ignorant
Uneducated in general; lacking knowledge or sophistication.

ignored
Intentionally disregarded.

ill
Affected by an impairment of normal physical or mental function; sick.

ill-humored
Brusque and surly and forbidding.

illicit
1. Contrary to or forbidden by law.
2. Contrary to accepted morality (especially sexual morality) or convention.

ill-tempered
Annoyed and irritable.

illuminated
Free from confusion or ambiguity; clear.

imaginative
Independent and creative in thought or action.

imbalanced
Out of equilibrium.

immaculate
Completely neat and clean.

immature
Not fully developed emotionally or intellectually.

immersed
Deeply involved in a specific activity or interest.

immobile
Unable to move.

immobilized
Not moving because of someone or something.

immodest
Having an exaggerated opinion of one's importance,
ability, etc.

immoral
Deliberately violating accepted principles of right and
wrong.

immortal
1. Living forever.
2. Enduring in fame.

immovable
Unable to be moved.

immune
Unaffected by a given influence.

impaired
Diminished in strength, quality, or utility; mentally or physically unfit.

impartial
Lacking favoritism; free from undue bias or preconceived opinions.

impassioned
Deeply excited, zealous, and interested; intensely enthusiastic.

impassive
Unaffected, detached; apathetic.

impatient
Restless and/or eager; short-tempered under delay or opposition.

impeccable
Without fault or error.

impeded
Having difficulty or slowness (with someone or something) caused by a hindrance or obstacle.

impelled
Urged or forced to action through moral pressure.

imperfect
Not perfect; defective or inadequate.

imperiled
Put in danger or threatened by something or someone.

imperious
Feeling arrogantly superior to and disdainful for those one views as unworthy.

impermanent
Existing for a limited time only.

impermeable
Impossible to penetrate or pass through.

impertinent
Disrespectful; rude.

imperturbable
Extremely calm and composed; not easily perturbed, excited, or upset.

impervious
Unable to be affected by something or someone.

impetuous
Impulsive; unduly hasty and lacking thought or deliberation.

impious
Lacking due respect or dutifulness.

impish
Naughtily or annoyingly playful.

implacable
Incapable of being appeased or pacified.

impolite
Without good manners.

important
1. Greatly significant or valuable.
2. Having authority, ascendancy, or influence.

importunate
Persistent to the point of annoyance.

imposing
Impressive in appearance; eminent.

impotent
Lacking power or ability.

impractical
1. Lacking sensibility about the reality of something.
2. Impossible to accomplish.

impressed
Deeply or markedly affected or influenced.

impressionable
Easily impressed or influenced.

impressive
Leaving a strong or vivid impression or having a strong effect.

imprisoned
Held in captivity; confined.

improper
Not suitable, right, or appropriate.

impudent
Casually disrespectful.

impugned
Attacked or disputed as false or wrong.

impulsive
Taking action without forethought.

impure
Immoral or obscene.

inaccessible
1. Capable of being reached only with great difficulty or not at all.
2. Not capable of being obtained.

inactive
Not active physically or mentally; lacking energy or will.

inadequate
Lacking requisite qualities or resources to meet a task.

inane
Extremely silly or stupid.

inappropriate
Unsuitable for a particular occasion.

inattentive
Lacking attention or care.

incapable
1. The absence of capacity or ability.
2. Lacking the temperament or inclination for something.

incapacitated
1. Unable to perform a certain action.
2. Lacking or deprived of strength or power.

incensed
Feeling outraged; angered because of an unjust act or something one believes to be wrong.

incited
Urged to take unlawful action.

inclined
Favorably disposed or willing.

incoherent
Unable to express oneself clearly or fluently.

incommunicative
Disinclined to talk, give information, or express opinions.

incompetent
Lacking skill or aptitude.

incomplete
Not yet finished.

inconceivable
Totally unlikely.

inconclusive
Unable to put an end to doubt or question about something.

incongruent
Incompatible with someone or something.

inconsiderate
Lacking regard for the rights or feelings of others.

inconsistent
Incapable of being consistent or harmonious.

inconsolable
Sad beyond comforting.

inconspicuous
Invisible; not prominent or readily noticeable.

inconvenienced
Troubled or bothered by someone or something.

inconvenient
Bothered by something that is not suited to one's comfort, purpose, or needs.

incorrect
Not in conformity with fact or truth.

incorrigible
Difficult or impossible to manage or control.

incredible
Beyond belief or understanding.

incredulity
Doubt about the truth of something.

incredulous
Indisposed or unwilling to believe.

inculcated
Taught and impressed on by frequent repetitions or admonitions.

indebted
Obligated to someone.

indecent
1. Nonconforming with accepted standards of what is right or proper in polite society.
2. Offensive to good taste, especially in sexual matters.

indecisive
Unable to make a decision or be firm.

indefinite
Vague or not clearly defined or stated.

independent
1. Neutral or uncommitted.
2. Free from external control and constraint.

indescribable
Unable to be defined or explained.

indestructible
Immune to destruction.

indicted
Formally accused of a crime.

indifferent
Completely lacking interest.

indifference
1. Unbiased, impartial unconcern.
2. Lack of enthusiasm or interest in things generally.

indignant
Angry about something unjust or wrong.

indignation
Righteous anger.

indirect
Not being straightforward.

indiscreet
Without discretion; injudicious.

indisposed
Unwell; unwilling.

indoctrinated
Imbued with education about a specific ideology,
principle, doctrine, point of view, etc.

indolent
Disinclined to work or exertion; slow or lazy.

indulged
Having enjoyed something excessively.

indulgent
Tolerant or lenient.

industrious
Perseverant and energetically hardworking; diligent.

inebriated
Intoxicated; drunk.

ineffective
Lacking the ability or skill to perform effectively; inadequate.

ineffectual
Unable to produce a result or effect.

inefficient
Unable to produce desired results; wasteful.

inept
Generally incompetent and ineffectual.

inequality
A lack of equality.

inert
Slow and apathetic.

inexorable
Impervious to pleas, persuasion, requests, or reason.

inexplicable
Incapable of being explained or accounted for.

infallible
Incapable of failure or error.

infamous
Known widely and usually unfavorably.

infantile
Lacking maturity.

infatuated
Intensely passionate; foolish or unreasonable fondness.

infected
1. Contaminated with a disease or microorganism.
2. Corrupt with ideas or an ideology.

infelicitous
Inappropriate, unhappy, or unfortunate.

inferior
Low in rank or importance.

infirm
Lacking firmness of will or character or purpose.

inflamed
Aroused and excited intensely about something or someone.

inflammatory
Inciting action or rebellion.

inflated
Enlarged beyond truth or reasonableness.

inflexible
Incapable of change.

influenced
Induced into action by someone's or something's capacity or power of influence.

influential
Having influence or power.

informal
Without formality; casual.

informed
Knowledgeable and/or educated.

infuriated
Angry; enraged.

infused
Filled with something—thoughts, ideas, ambition, etc.

ingenious
Inventive and skillful.

ingenuity
The power of creative imagination.

ingenuous
1. Unable to mask one's feelings; not devious.
2. Lacking sophistication or worldliness.

ingratiated
Favoring somebody because of their deliberately pleasing efforts.

inhibited
Restrained, self-conscious; unable to act.

inhospitable
Unfriendly and unwelcoming.

inhuman
Cruel with no compassion; cold; nonhuman.

inhumane
Lacking pity or compassion.

inimical
Not friendly.

initiative
Readiness to embark on bold new ventures.

injured
Emotionally hurt, upset, or annoyed.

innocent
Free from evil or guilt.

innovative
1. Ahead of the times.
2. Being or producing something like nothing done, experienced, or created before.

inoculated
Having had a new idea or attitude introduced into one's mind by someone or something.

inquisitive
Curious about someone or something.

insane
Afflicted with or characteristic of mental derangement.

insanity
A relatively permanent disorder of the mind.

insatiable
Impossible to satisfy.

inscrutable
Difficult to understand.

insecure
Lacking self-confidence; feeling unsafe.

insecurity
1. Anxiety from experiencing vulnerability.
2. Subject to danger or injury.

insensitive
Without concern for others' feelings.

insight
Clear or deep perception of a situation.

insightful
Clearly and deeply perceptive.

insignificant
Devoid of importance, meaning, or force.

insincere
Lacking sincerity.

insistent
Demanding without accepting refusal.

insolent
Rude and disrespectful.

insouciant
Blithely unconcerned; indifferent.

inspiration
Arousal of the mind to do something creative, special, or unusual.

inspirational
Inspiring to someone.

inspired
Impulsively creative; excited.

instilled
Having an idea, attitude, and/or quality gradually established in one's mind and/or nature.

instructive
Informative or enlightening to others.

insubordinate
Disposed to or engaged in defiance of established authority.

insubstantial
Lacking strength or solidity; unreal.

insufficient
Unable to fulfill a need or requirement.

insulted
Offended; abused.

insurgent
In opposition to a civil authority or government.

intact
Undamaged in any way; complete.

intellectual
Characterized by intelligence rather than emotions or instinct.

intelligent
Having a capacity for thought and reason, especially to a high degree.

intense
Distinctive in a feature or experience to a heightened degree.

intent
An anticipated outcome that guides one's planned actions.

interested
Curious, fascinated, or concerned about someone or something.

interference
An obstruction, imposition, or hindrance caused by someone or something.

interrelated
Reciprocally connected.

interrogated
Questioned aggressively.

interrupted
Intermittently interfered with or disrupted in an activity by someone or something.

intimate
1. Deeply private and personal.
2. Marked by close acquaintance, association, or familiarity.

intimidated
Timid or fearful.

intimidating
Threatening or scary.

intolerant
Unwilling to tolerate differences of opinion.

intoxicated
Lacking control from overconsumption; excited or exhilarated.

intrepid
Fearless; brave.

intrigue
A crafty and involved plot to achieve one's (usually sinister) ends.

intrigued
Interested or curious.

introspective
Reflecting on one's own sensory and perceptual experiences.

introverted
Focused inward toward the self.

intrusive
Disruptive and annoying.

intuitive
Recognizing or identifying something from instinct rather than from reasoning or observation.

inundated
Overwhelmed from a deluge of something.

invalidated
Deprived of legal force.

inventive
Original and capable of creating or designing something new.

invidious
Discriminatory and unjust.

invigorated
Restored with energy.

invisible
1. Impossible or nearly impossible to see; imperceptible to the eye.
2. Unnoticeable by others.

invited
Welcome and included.

inviting
Attractive and tempting.

involved
Connected by participation, association, or use.

invulnerable
Immune to attack; impregnable.

irascible
Angry; irritable.

irate
Extremely angry.

ireful
Extremely angry.

irked
Irritated by someone or something.

irrational
Lacking reason.

irregular
Deviating from normal expectations; somewhat odd, strange, or abnormal.

irreligious
Hostile or indifferent to religion.

irrepressible
Impossible to repress or control.

irreproachable
Free of guilt; not subject to blame.

irresistible
Overpoweringly attractive.

irresolute
Uncertain how to act or proceed.

irresponsible
Lacking care for consequences.

irreverent
Lacking due respect or veneration.

irritable
Easily irritated or annoyed.

irritated
Impatient and/or angry.

irritation
Annoyance caused by someone or something.

isolated
Set or kept apart from others.

itchy
Nervous and unable to relax.

jaded
Having a loss of interest or being bored with something or somebody (usually through overuse or overexposure).

jaundiced
Prejudiced, envious, or showing distaste.

jaunty
Cheerful and self-confident.

jazzed
Excited and/or enthusiastic about something.

jealous
Painfully desirous of another's advantages.

jealousy
Envy for someone or something (especially for a rival).

jeopardized
Put at risk.

jilted
Rejected; abandoned.

jinxed
Foredoomed to failure.

jittery
Tense and/or edgy.

jocular
Good-humored.

jolly
High-spirited and merry.

jolted
Disturbed psychologically as if by a physical jolt or shock.

jovial
Cheerful and friendly.

joy
Great happiness.

joyful
Full of high-spirited delight.

joyless
Grim or dismal.

joyous
Happy and joyful.

jubilant
Joyful and proud.

judged
Evaluated by someone.

judgmental
Having an excessive or strong point of view.

judicious
Having good judgment or common sense in practical matters.

juiced
Intoxicated; drunk.

juicy
Strongly sexually appealing.

jumbled
Mixed up.

jumpy
Tense and edgy.

just
1. Free from favoritism, self-interest, bias, or deception.
2. Conforming with established standards or rules; morally excellent.

justified
Supported with proof.

keen
Eager or enthusiastic.

kept
Controlled by one whose money provides support.

kidded
Feeling fooled with false information for fun.

kind
Characterized by a tender, considerate, and helpful nature.

kindhearted
Having sympathy that arises from a kind heart.

kindly
Pleasant and agreeable.

kindness
An innately kind disposition.

kingly
Having the rank of, resembling, or befitting a king.

kinky
Bizarre or deviant in tastes.

kittenish
Playful like a lively kitten.

knackered
Very tired.

knavish
Skillfully deceptive.

knightly
Attentive to women like an ideal knight.

knowledgeable
Thoroughly acquainted with something through study or experience.

known
Perceived as familiar.

kooky
Mentally irregular; eccentric.

labeled
Judged or categorized.

labile
Liable to change.

lackadaisical
Careless and lazy.

lackluster
Without brilliance or vitality.

laconic
Brief and to the point.

lambasted
Harshly criticized.

lament
To have grief or sorrow; to mourn.

lamenting
Grieving or sorrowful.

lampooned
Ridiculed with satire.

languid
Lacking spirit or liveliness.

lascivious
Lustful and desirous.

late
At or toward an end period or stage of development; delayed.

laughable
Absurdly amusing.

lavish
Extremely generous or luxurious.

lavished
Treated with extravagance.

lax
1. Lacking rigor or strictness.
2. Relaxed and/or loose.

lazy
Disinclined to work or exertion.

lecherous
Given to excessive indulgence in sexual activity.

led
Guided or influenced by someone or something.

leery
Openly distrustful and unwilling to confide.

legitimate
Authentic, authorized, and genuine.

lethargic
Slow, sluggish, and apathetic.

levelheaded
Having good judgment.

levity
Inappropriate lack of seriousness.

lewd
Preoccupied with lustful desires; morally loose.

liable
Responsible, legally or otherwise.

liberal
1. Favoring progress and reform and the protection of civil liberties.
2. Broad-minded.
3. Tolerant of change; not bound by authoritarianism, orthodoxy, or tradition.

liberated
Free from traditional social restraints.

libertine
Morally unrestrained.

libidinous
Lustful and desirous.

licentious
Promiscuous and unrestrained morally.

lifeless
Lacking animation or excitement.

lifelike
Free from artificiality.

lifted
Having raised spirits or confidence.

light
Free from sadness or troubles.

lighthearted
Carefree and happy.

likable
Easy to like; agreeable.

like
Satisfaction and enjoyment.

liked
Attractive or pleasant to others.

limited
Restricted in ability or capacity.

limp
Without energy or will.

lionhearted
Extraordinarily courageous.

listless
Low in energy; lacking enthusiasm.

litigious
Characterized by an inclination to dispute or disagree, even to engage in lawsuits.

lively
Full of life and energy.

liverish
Irritable, as if suffering from indigestion.

livid
Furiously angry.

loath
Unwilling to do something contrary to one's custom.

loathe
To intensely dislike.

loathed
Extremely distasteful and rejected by others.

loathsome
Highly offensive; arousing aversion or disgust.

lofty
With great dignity or nobility.

logical
Capable of thinking and expressing oneself in a clear and consistent manner.

lonely
Lacking companions or companionship; alone.

lonesome
1. Single and isolated from others.
2. Dejected from being alone.

longing
Prolonged unfulfilled desire or need.

loneliness
Sadness resulting from being forsaken or abandoned.

loopy
Mentally irregular.

loose
1. Free, open, and relaxed.
2. Casual and unrestrained in sexual behavior.
3. Lacking a sense of restraint or responsibility; careless.

loss
Grief associated with being deprived of someone or something.

lost
Confused or insecure; deeply absorbed in thought.

loud
Tastelessly showy.

lousy
Very bad.

lovable
Attractive and affectionate.

love
A deep romantic and/or sexual attraction to someone; an intense affection or devotion.

loved
Held dear by others.

loveless
Without love.

lovelorn
Unhappy in love; suffering from unrequited love.

lovely
Appealing to the emotions as well as the eye.

lovesick
Suffering and weak because of love for another.

lovesome
Warm and affectionate.

love struck
Affected by sudden and intense romantic love.

loving
Feeling love and affection.

low
1. Deficient of vital energy.
2. Depressed.
3. Submissive.

lowly
Low or inferior in station or quality.

low-spirited
1. Filled with melancholy and despondency.
2. Depressed; deficient of vital energy.

loyal
Devoted to someone or something; allegiant.

loyalty
Allegiance to someone or something.

lubricious
Lustful in an intentional and/or offensive way.

luckless
Having bad luck; misfortunate.

lucky
Fortunate; willing to take risks.

ludicrous
Broadly or extravagantly humorous; resembling farce.

lukewarm
Having little interest or enthusiasm.

luminous
1. Radiant with energy.
2. Intellectually bright; enlightened.

lured
Provoked to do something through (often false or exaggerated) promises or persuasion.

lustful
Driven by strong desire.

lusty
Vigorously passionate.

macho
Proud of one's masculinity.

mad
1. Roused to anger.
2. Affected with insanity.
3. Very foolish.

magical
1. Extraordinarily beautiful and delightful, as if caused by magic.
2. Having supernatural powers.

magnificent
Grand and/or excellent.

maimed
Wounded, crippled, or disabled.

maladjusted
Emotionally unstable and having difficulty coping with personal relationships.

malaise
Discomfort, uneasiness, or depression.

malcontent
Discontented, as toward authority.

malevolent
Having evil ill will toward others; hatred.

malicious
Intending to do harm; cruel.

malignant
Dangerous to health.

maligned
Unfavorably spoken about.

malleable
Easily influenced.

malnourished
Suffering from insufficient quality or quantity of nourishment.

manageable
Capable of being managed or controlled.

managerial
Responsible for management-like duties.

mangled
Feeling injured severely.

manhandled
Handled roughly.

maniacal
Wildly disordered.

manic
Affected with or marked by frenzy or mania, uncontrolled by reason.

manipulable
Easily managed (controlled, taught, or molded).

manipulated
Deviously or shrewdly controlled or influenced.

manipulative
Skillful in influencing or controlling others to one's own advantage.

manly
Having qualities befitting a man.

marginalized
1. Relegated to a lower or outer edge, as of specific groups of people.
2. Made to be insignificant by someone or something.

marred
Blemished by injury or rough wear.

married
1. Joined in matrimony.
2. United together with someone or something.

marveling
Amazed, astonished, and/or surprised.

marvelous
Extraordinarily good or great.

masochistic
Deriving pleasure or sexual gratification from being abused or dominated.

masterful
Supreme mastery or skill.

materialistic
Deeply concerned with material objects and/or money.

maternal
Characteristic of a mother.

mature
Fully developed or fully grown.

maudlin
Excessively sentimental, usually with drunkenness.

mawkish
Effusive or insincere in emotion.

meager
Deficient in amount, quality, or extent.

mean
Malicious or lacking generosity.

mechanical
Lacking spontaneity or thought; automatic.

meddlesome
Intrusive in a meddling or offensive manner.

medicated
Affected by a medicinal substance.

mediocre
Moderate to inferior in quality.

meditative
Deeply or seriously thoughtful.

meek
Humble; retiringly mild and/or submissive.

megalomaniacal
Suffering from delusions of grandeur.

melancholic
Greatly sad; depressed.

melancholy
Deep, thoughtful sadness.

melded
Blended or mixed together with something.

mellow
Soft, relaxed, easygoing, genial, and/or unhurried.

melodramatic
Having the excitement and emotional appeal of melodrama.

menaced
Exposed to hostility.

menacing
Threatening and hostile.

mental
Having a disorder of the mind.

mercenary
Profit-oriented.

merciful
Showing great kindness toward the distressed; gracious.

mercurial
Erratic; unpredictable.

mercy
Kindness, compassion, and leniency from someone or something.

merriness
Merry joking.

merry
Cheerful and joyous.

mesmerized
Strongly attracted; fascinated.

messy
Dirty and disorderly.

methodical
Orderly or systematic.

meticulous
Taking extreme care in treatment of details.

micromanaged
Controlled with excessive attention to detail.

miffed
Aroused to impatience or anger.

mighty
Great in strength, force, or intensity.

mild
Moderate in type, degree, effect, or force; far from extreme.

militant
Disposed to warfare or hard-line policies.

mindful
Conscious or aware of something.

mindless
Devoid of intelligence or thought.

minimized
Small or insignificant.

miraculous
Peculiarly fortunate as if by miracle or magic.

mirth
Amusement; joy.

mirthful
High-spirited and merry.

mirthless
Lacking amusement.

misanthropic
Displaying the worst of human nature and motives; having a sneering disbelief in humanity.

mischievous
Desiring to cause harm in a playful way.

misdiagnosed
Incorrectly identified as having something, such as an illness, ailment, or disease.

miserable
Very unhappy; full of misery.

miserly
Lacking generosity.

misgiving
A doubt about someone's honesty.

misguided
Led in the wrong direction.

misinformed
Falsely informed; misled.

misinterpreted
Interpreted in the wrong way.

misjudged
Judged incorrectly.

misled
Led in the wrong direction.

misrepresented
Portrayed incorrectly.

missed
Noticeably absent from something.

mistaken
Wrong in opinion or judgment.

mistreated
Subjected to cruel treatment.

mistrust
Doubt about someone's honesty.

mistrusted
Regarded as untrustworthy; regarded with suspicion.

mistrustful
Openly distrustful and unwilling to confide in another.

misunderstood
Wrongly understood.

misused
Used incorrectly, carelessly, or for an improper purpose.

mobilized
Ready for action or use.

mocked
Imitated with mockery and derision.

moderate
Within reasonable or average limits; not excessive or extreme.

modern
Contemporary in style, ideas, fashion, and design.

modest
1. Humble in spirit or manner.
2. Sexually inoffensive.

modesty
Freedom from vanity or conceit.

molded
Influenced to fit or integrate with something.

molested
Sexually harassed or assaulted.

mollified
More favorably inclined; appeased.

mollycoddled
Treated with excessive indulgence.

monitored
Under surveillance.

monomaniacal
Obsessed with a single subject or idea.

monopolized
Being exclusively or fully occupied or controlled by someone or something.

monotonous
Tediously repetitious or lacking in variety.

monotony
Wearisome constancy, routine, and lack of variety.

monstrous
1. Shockingly brutal or cruel.
2. Abnormally large.
3. Distorted and unnatural in shape or size; abnormal and hideous.

moody
Sharply varying moods; gloomy.

mopey
Low in spirits; depressed.

moral
Concerned with principles of right and wrong or conforming to standards of behavior and character based on those principles.

moralistic
Narrowly and conventionally moral.

morbid
Unhealthy in mental state, usually related to death or other disturbing things.

mordant
Harshly ironic or sinister.

moribund
Near the point of death.

moronic
Characteristic of a mental age between eight and twelve years.

morose
Sullen and ill-tempered.

mortified
Embarrassed, ashamed, or humiliated.

mothered
Cared for by one's mother or as if by one's mother.

motherless
Not having a living or known mother.

motherly
Befitting of a mother; warm and nurturing.

motivated
Provided with or given incentive to take action.

motivation
Arousal to action toward a desired goal; the reason for action; that which gives purpose and direction to behavior.

mournful
Sorrowful, sad.

mourning
Sorrowful through loss or deprivation.

mouthy
Inclined to speak frequently.

moved
1. Provoked or influenced to change.
2. Emotionally affected.

muddled
Mixed up or confused.

mulish
Stubborn; unreasonably rigid in the face of argument, entreaty, or attack.

mummified
Like a mummy—lifeless, dried up, and wrapped up.

murky
Dark or gloomy; unclear.

mushy
Excessively sentimental.

musical
Talented in or devoted to music or capable of producing music.

mutinous
Rebellious against authority.

muzzled
Prevented from speaking out.

mysterious
Difficult to understand or interpret; obscure in nature.

mystical
Unapparent to the senses of others nor obvious to the intelligence; beyond ordinary understanding.

mystified
Totally perplexed and mixed up.

nagged
Constantly urged, usually to the point of annoyance.

nailed
Apprehended or exposed for being or doing something wrong.

naive
Characterized by unaffected simplicity and lack of guile or worldly experience.

naked
Completely exposed; devoid of elaboration or diminution or concealment; bare and pure.

namby-pamby
Weak in willpower, courage, or vitality.

nameless
Unknown or anonymous.

narcissistic
1. Having an inflated sense of one's own importance.
2. Characterized by excessive love of oneself;
egocentric; egoistic.

narrow-minded
Lacking tolerance, flexibility, or breadth of view.

nasty
Offensive, indecent, or malicious.

natural
1. Talented through inherited qualities.
2. Free from artificiality.

naughty
Disobedient and/or suggestive of sexual impropriety.

nauseated
Upset, sick; about to vomit.

neat
Clean or organized.

necessary
Absolutely essential.

needed
Necessary for relief, service, or supply.

needled
Annoyed or provoked, as by constant criticism.

needy
Poor or helpless enough to need assistance.

negated
Proven negative; shown to be false.

negative
Characterized by negation, denial, opposition, or resistance.

negativity
Habitual skepticism and a disagreeable tendency to deny, oppose, or resist suggestions or commands.

neglected
Ignored, disregarded; suffering from lack of care and attention.

neglectful
Caring improperly for someone or something.

negligent
Neglectful and showing an undue lack of concern.

nerdy
Intelligent and usually obsessed with (and an expert of) a specific topic.

nerve
1. The courage to carry on.
2. Impudent aggressiveness.

nervous
Anxious; easily agitated.

nervy
1. Edgy and tense.
2. Offensively bold.
3. Courageous and contemptuous of danger.

nestled
Positioned comfortably and cozily.

nettled
Annoyed or irritated.

neurotic
Affected with an emotional disorder.

neutral
Feeling no personal preference.

nice
Feeling pleasant, pleasing, or agreeable in nature or appearance.

nifty
Very good.

nihilism
The philosophy that everything is not real; complete denial of all established authority and institutions.

nihilistic
In complete denial of all established authority and institutions.

nimble
Mentally and/or physically quick.

nitpicked
Highly criticized over minor details.

nitpicky
Overly critical; criticizing of minor details.

noble
1. Dignified and/or stately.
2. Morally elevated in character.

noisy
Attractive because of showiness or bright colors.

nomadic
Migratory; highly mobile.

nonchalance
A casual lack of concern.

nonchalant
Casual; blithely unconcerned; calm and relaxed.

noncommittal
Unwilling to bind oneself to a particular course of action or view or the like.

nonconforming
Unwilling to conform to established customs or doctrines, especially in religion.

nonexistent
Absent from existence, being, or actuality.

nonplused
Filled with bewilderment.

normal
Adhering to a norm, standard, level, type, or social construct; not abnormal.

nostalgic
1. Unhappy about being away and longing for familiar things or persons.
2. Fond of an earlier time.

nosy
Offensively curious or inquisitive.

nothing
No measurable emotion.

noticed
Perceived or observed by someone or something.

nourished
Provided with adequate sustenance.

nudged
Pushed into action by pestering or gentle annoyance.

nullified
Made ineffective or insignificant.

numb
Insensitive; lacking sensation; feeling nothing.

numbed
Feeling a loss of sensation.

numbness
A lack of enthusiasm for or lack of interest in things generally.

nursed
Treated with special, nurturing care.

nuts
Mentally irregular; crazy.

nutty
Acting mentally irregular; crazy.

nymphomaniacal
Having excessive sexual desire.

obedient
Dutifully compliant with the commands or instructions of those in authority.

obeyed
Experiencing obedience from another.

objectified
Treated as impersonal or presented as an object.

obligated
Bound or committed to something.

obliged
Under a moral obligation to do something.

obliterated
Reduced to nothingness.

oblivious
Lacking conscious awareness.

obnoxious
Vulgar and objectionable.

obscene
Offensive; morally loose.

obsequious
Attentive in an ingratiating or servile manner.

observant
Quick to notice; having quick and keen perception.

observed
Closely watched.

obsessed
Excessively or compulsively concerned with something.

obsessive
Having an inclination to compulsivity.

obstinate
Resistant to guidance or discipline.

obstructed
Shut off to passage or view or hindered from action.

obvious
Easily perceived by the senses or grasped by the mind.

odd
Beyond or deviating from the usual or expected.

odious
Unequivocally detestable.

off
Unpalatable or in an abnormal state.

offended
1. Hurt, upset, or annoyed.
2. Resentful or indignant.
3. Insulted by someone or something.

offensive
Unpleasant or disgusting, especially to the senses.

officious
Intrusive in a meddling or offensive manner.

ogreish
Cruel and wicked.

okay
Satisfactory or in satisfactory condition.

old
Having lived for a relatively long time or attained a specific age.

old-fashioned
Traditional in style, ideas, fashion, and design.

ominous
Responsible for indicating that something evil or unpleasant is going to happen; threatening.

omnipotent
Unlimited in power.

on
Ready to function; effective.

open
1. Ready or willing to receive something favorably.
2. Straightforward and direct without reserve or secretiveness.

open-minded
Ready to entertain new ideas.

opinionated
Obstinate in one's opinions.

opportunistic
Ready to take immediate advantage, often unethically, of any circumstance of possible benefit.

opposed
Against or resistant to someone or something.

opposition
Contrast or resistance from someone or something.

oppositional
Inclined to resist.

oppressed
Distressed, anxious, or uncomfortable from burden.

oppressive
Cruel and brutal in order to cause hardship and constraint for someone or something.

optimism
A disposition that all is going to turn out well.

optimistic
Positive, hopeful, and confident about the future.

opulent
Ostentatiously rich and superior in quality.

orderly
Devoid of violence or disruption.

ordinary
Commonplace; not exceptional in any way, especially in quality, ability, size, or degree.

organized
Structured and/or orderly and efficient in arrangement or function.

ornery
Angry and combative.

orphaned
Deprived of parents by death or desertion.

ostentatious
Tawdry or vulgar with intention to attract attention.

ostracized
Expelled from a community or group.

ousted
Removed and replaced.

outcast
Rejected or excluded from society or one's home.

outdated
Old; no longer valid or fashionable.

outdone
Bested by someone or something.

outgoing
Friendly, confident, and typically ready to lead or participate in something.

outlandish
Conspicuously or grossly unconventional or unusual.

outnumbered
Exceeded in numbers.

outraged
Intensely angered, shocked, and/or indignant.

outrageous
1. Grossly offensive to decency or morality; causing horror.
2. Greatly exceeding bounds of reason or moderation.

outranked
Surpassed by others in rank.

outspoken
Given to expressing oneself freely or insistently.

outstanding
1. Very good.
2. Distinguished from others in excellence.

overanxious
Anxious or nervous to an excessive degree.

overbearing
Acting arrogant and superior to and disdainful of those one views as unworthy; domineering.

overburdened
Having an excessive load of responsibilities, work, or cares.

overcome
Defeated; overwhelmed.

overconfident
Excessively confident.

overdrawn
Enlarged beyond bounds or beyond the truth.

overestimated
Unable or incapable of meeting an estimate or expectation.

overexcited
Excessively excited.

overflowing
Experiencing an excessive flow or extreme amount of something, such as emotion.

overjoyed
Extremely joyful or happy.

overloaded
Loaded past capacity.

overlooked
Not taken into account.

overpowered
Overcome by superior force.

overprotected
Excessively safe.

overruled
Rejected or ruled against.

oversensitive
Unduly sensitive or thin-skinned.

oversimplified
Easy or simple to an excessive degree.

overstimulated
Experiencing excessive exposure to the senses; invigorated.

overwhelmed
Feeling overcome or engulfed by something, such as an emotion.

overworked
Excessively used or active.

overwrought
Deeply agitated, especially from excessive and strong emotions.

overzealous
Excessively enthusiastic for and intensely devoted to a cause or idea.

owed
Be indebted to.

owned
Possessed or belonging to another.

ownership
Responsibility for and/or possession of something.

pacified
Experiencing peace and goodwill, usually from the positive actions of someone or something; appeased.

pain
Discomfort, anguish, and/or misery.

pained
Emotionally hurt, upset, or annoyed.

paired
Mated sexually.

pampered
Treated with excessive indulgence.

panic
Overwhelming fear and anxiety.

panicked
Thrown into a state of intense fear or desperation.

panicky
Intensely afraid or desperate.

paralyzed
Numb; unable to function.

paranoia
Delusions of persecution or grandeur.

paranoid
Suffering from undue suspicion.

parasitic
Characteristic of a parasite or leech.

pardoned
Forgiven or excused of something.

parsimonious
Excessively unwilling to spend.

partial
Having a strong preference or liking for; biased.

passion
1. A strong feeling or emotion.
2. Strong sexual desire.

passionate
Having strong emotions and/or beliefs.

passive
1. Lacking energy or will; inactive.
2. Peacefully resistant.

pastoral
Characteristic of idealized country life; idyllically rustic.

pat
1. Exactly suited to the occasion.
2. Complete or situated perfectly.

paternal
Characteristic of a father.

pathetic
Deserving of or inciting pity.

patience
Good-natured tolerance of delay or incompetence.

patient
Having endurance for trying circumstances with an even temper.

patriotic
Inspired by love for one's country.

patronized
Treated condescendingly.

peace
1. The absence of mental stress or anxiety.
2. Harmonious relations; freedom from disputes.
3. Uninterrupted stillness.

peaceful
Undisturbed by strife, turmoil, or war; tranquil.

peachy
Very good.

peckish
Somewhat hungry.

peculiar
Beyond or deviating from the usual or expected;
unique.

pedantic
Having a narrow focus on or display of learning,
especially its trivial aspects.

pedestrian
Lacking wit or imagination.

peeved
Annoyed, irritated, or resentful.

peevish
Easily irritated or annoyed by unimportant things.

pell-mell
Confusion or disorder.

penetrable
Capable of being penetrated.

penitent
Remorseful for misdeeds.

pensive
Deeply reflective or in serious thought.

peppy
Energetic and lively.

perceived
Understood or detected by means of the senses.

perceptive
Having the ability to perceive or understand; keen in discernment.

peremptory
Ending all debate or action.

perfect
1. Complete and without defect or blemish.
2. Precisely accurate or exact.
3. Very good.

perfectionistic
Displeased by anything that does not meet very high standards.

perilous
Fraught with danger.

peripheral
Related to the key issue but not of central importance.

perky
Lively and lighthearted.

permanence
Ability to exist for an indefinite duration.

permanent
1. Continuing or enduring without marked change in status, condition, or place.
2. Incapable of being reversed or returned to the original condition.

permeable
Capable of absorbing something, such as thoughts or ideas.

permissive
Inclined to grant permission; allowing.

permitted
Allowed to do something.

perplexed
Full of difficulty, confusion, or bewilderment.

persecuted
Subjected to hostility and cruelty.

persistent
Stubbornly unyielding.

persnickety
Excessively precise and attentive to trivial details.

perspicuous
Transparently clear; easily understandable.

persuaded
Convinced by someone or something to adopt a certain position, belief, or course of action.

persuasive
Having the power to induce action or belief.

pert
Lively and attractive.

pertinacious
Stubbornly unyielding.

pertinent
Precisely or logically relevant to the matter at hand.

perturbed
Feeling uneasy or worried or alarmed; upset.

perverse
Opposing and contradictory; resistant to guidance or discipline.

perverted
Corrupt morally or by intemperance or sensuality.

pervious
Open to allowing something to happen or pass through.

pessimistic
Expecting the worst possible outcome.

pestered
Troubled persistently, especially with petty annoyances.

petered out
Having depleted all of one's strength and energy until all activity has ceased.

petrified
Dazed and stunned from fright; afraid.

petty
1. Inferior in rank or status.
2. Small and of little importance.

petulant
Easily irritated or annoyed or childishly sulky.

phenomenal
Exceedingly or unbelievably great.

philanthropic
Generous in assistance to someone, something, or a group.

phlegmatic
Having little emotion; calm or sluggish.

phobic
Suffering from irrational fears.

phony
Fraudulent; having a misleading appearance.

physical
Relating to the body as distinguished from the mind or the spirit.

picked apart
Meticulously criticized.

picked on
Bullied or made fun of.

picky
Exacting, especially about details.

pierced
Deeply or sharply moved emotionally.

pigeonholed
1. Placed into a specific category or situation.
2. Stereotyped or categorized unfairly.

pillaged
Robbed and destroyed by force and violence.

pine
To desire something or someone who is not present.

pining
Deeply longing.

pious
Reverent to a deity.

piquant
Engagingly stimulating or provocative.

piqued
Resentful or indignant; stimulated.

pissed
Aroused to impatience or anger.

pissed off
Very angry.

pissy
Annoying, arrogant, and argumentative.

piteous
Deserving of or inciting pity.

pitied
Receiving compassion from someone, usually for a negative situation.

pitiful
Sad, unfortunate, and miserable.

pitiless
Without mercy; deficient in humane and kindly feelings.

pity
Sympathy and sorrow for the misfortunes of others.

placated
Having been influenced from anger to calm by someone or something.

placid
Not easily irritated.

plagued
Chronically annoyed by someone or something.

plain
1. Lacking physical beauty or proportion.
2. Simple; without embellishment or ornamentation.

plaintive
Sorrowful; mournful.

planless
Aimlessly drifting.

platonic
1. Affectionate without romantic desire.
2. Free from physical desire.

played
Foolishly deceived by the antics of another.

playful
Fun and joyful.

pleasant
Pleasing; in harmony with one's taste or likings.

pleased
Experiencing or manifesting pleasure.

pleasure
1. Agreeable sensations or emotions.
2. The excitement, relish, or happiness produced by the expectation or the enjoyment of something good, delightful, or satisfying.

pleasured
1. Sexually stimulated.
2. Filled with excitement and joy and/or happiness and satisfaction.

pliable
Susceptible to being led or directed.

pliant
Capable of being influenced or formed.

plumbed
Probed for knowledge about something.

plundered
Feeling a loss from being pillaged; robbed.

plush
Extravagant and profuse.

poignant
Arousing an effect.

poised
Balanced and ready for action.

poisoned
Spoiled or harmed by something or someone who is toxic.

poisonous
Having deep ill will; deliberately harmful.

polite
Experiencing regard for others through manners, speech, behavior, etc.

polluted
Rendered unwholesome by contaminants and pollution.

pompous
Puffed up with vanity; self-important.

pooped
Very tired.

poor
Insufficient in quantity to meet a need.

popular
Regarded with great favor, approval, or affection, especially by the general public.

porous
Able to absorb.

portentous
Ominously prophetic.

positive
Affirmative, accepting, or certain, etc.

possessed
Influenced or controlled by a powerful force, such as a strong emotion.

possessive
Having a desire to control or dominate.

potent
Possessing great influence.

pouty
Lightheartedly angry or sad.

poverty
The state of having little or no money and few or no material possessions.

powerful
Great in power, force, potency, or effect.

powerless
Lacking control, ability, influence, or power.

practical
1. Guided by experience and observation rather than theory.
2. Concerned with actual use or practice.

pragmatic
Guided by practical experience and observation rather than theory.

praised
Feeling approval by others.

precarious
Fraught with danger.

precious
Held dear and cared for deeply; cute.

precluded
Kept from doing or completing something.

precocious
Exceptionally early in development or maturity.

predatory
Having the desire to exploit, oppress, or otherwise victimize others.

predilection
A predisposition in favor of something; a strong liking.

prefer
To favor one thing over another.

preoccupied
Deeply absorbed in thought.

prepared
Ready or fit or suitable beforehand.

preppy
Influenced by or embodying a preparatory-school student's style and fashion.

pressed
Feeling pressure to take a specific action.

pressure
Distress or anxiety from persuasion, influence, intimidation, urgency, or expectation.

pressured
Urged to do something.

presumptuous
Excessively forward.

pretentious
Creating and maintaining an appearance of undeserved importance or distinction.

pretty
Pleasing by delicacy or grace; not imposing.

preyed on
Victimized; defenseless.

pride
Self-respect and personal worth.

prideful
Filled with arrogant superiority to and disdain for those one views as unworthy.

prim
Affectedly dainty or refined.

primal
1. In the earliest or original stage or state.
2. Essential to something.

primary
First in rank, importance, or value; direct and immediate rather than secondary.

primitive
1. Little evolved from or characteristic of an earlier ancestral type.
2. Lacking formal training; simple or naive in style.

primness
Excessive or affected modesty.

prissy
Exaggeratedly proper.

pristine
Completely free from dirt or contamination.

private
1. Deeply personal.
2. Kept to oneself.

privileged
Blessed with privileges.

privy
Informed about something secret or not generally known.

prized
Held in high regard.

proactive
Taking control of a situation by causing something to happen rather than waiting to respond to it after it happens.

probed
Questioned or examined thoroughly and closely.

prodigal
Recklessly wasteful.

prodigious
Great in size, force, or extent as to elicit awe.

productive
Capable of producing (especially abundantly).

profane
Disrespectful toward something that is sacred.

professional
Engaged and skilled in a specific profession or livelihood.

profligate
Recklessly wasteful.

progressing
Developing in a positive way.

progressive
Favoring and promoting progress; advancing.

prohibited
Excluded from use or mention.

promiscuous
Casual and unrestrained in sexual behavior.

promised
Expectation from a commitment made by someone.

promoted
Elevated to a higher position.

prompt
1. Ready and willing or quick to act.
2. With little or no delay; on time.

propagandistic
Characterized by spreading information for the purpose of promoting some cause.

propagandized
Subjected to propaganda.

propelled
Caused by force to move forward.

proper
1. Marked by suitability, rightness, or appropriateness.
2. Appropriate for a condition, purpose, occasion, or a person's character/needs.

propitiation
Appeasement (especially for God or a deity).

prosaic
Lacking wit or imagination.

prosecuted
Brought to trial for criminal action.

prosperous
1. Moderately rich.
2. Marked by peace and prosperity.

prostituted
Sold for money.

protected
Kept safe or defended from danger or injury or loss.

protective
Desiring and intending to protect someone or something.

proud
1. Self-respectful or pleased in something by which one measures self-worth.
2. Dignified or noble.

provincial
1. Rural; from the country.
2. Deeply associated with a province.

provocative
Intention to provoke, excite, or stimulate.

provoked
Incited, especially deliberately, to anger.

prowess
1. Expert skill in something.
2. Exceptional courage.

prudish
Exaggeratedly proper.

prurient
Excessively interested in sex; lustful.

psyched
Mentally prepared; feeling anticipation and excitement.

psychedelic
Characterized by intense and distorted perceptions, hallucinations, and feelings of euphoria or sometimes despair.

psychopathic
Suffering from a mental disorder.

psychotic
Afflicted with a severe mental disorder in which contact with reality is lost or highly distorted.

puckish
Annoyingly playful; mischievous.

puerile
Lacking maturity.

pugnacious
Ready and able to resort to force or violence.

pulled
1. Attracted to something.
2. Moved toward something in particular.

pulverized
Completely destroyed.

pumped
Tense with excitement and enthusiasm, as if from a rush of adrenaline.

punctual
Exact in timeliness; on time.

punished
Subjected to a penalty (such as pain, shame, restraint, or loss) for an offense or fault or in order to coerce some behavior (as a confession or obedience).

puny
Inferior in strength or significance.

pure
1. Without faults; sinless.
2. Free of extraneous elements of any kind.

purged
1. Made pure or free from sin or guilt.
2. Ousted from somewhere or something.

purposeful
Meaningful through having an aim.

pursuant
In conformance to or agreement with something.

pursued
Followed with enmity, as if to harm.

pushed
Forced to move or take action.

pushy
Aggressive ambition, energy, and initiative.

pusillanimous
Lacking in courage, strength, and resolution; contemptibly fearful.

puzzled
Filled with bewilderment; unable to understand; confused.

quaint
Strange in an interesting or pleasing way.

qualified
1. Properly trained for an office or position or task.
2. Appropriate for something.

quandary
Uncertainty or perplexity, especially as requiring a choice between equally unfavorable options.

quarantined
Placed into enforced isolation.

quarrelsome
Angry and/or disagreeing, with a desire to quarrel or fight.

quashed
Put down by force or intimidation.

queasy
Fraught with anxiety.

queenly
Having the rank of, resembling, or befitting a queen.

queer
1. Beyond or deviating from the usual or expected.
2. Having homosexual desires.

quenched
Satisfied or fulfilled of a need (a figurative thirst).

queried
Questioned for validity or accuracy.

questioned
Feeling challenged by someone about the accuracy, probity, or propriety of something.

quick
1. Easily aroused or excited.
2. Accomplished rapidly and without delay.
3. Fast in intelligence and/or agility.

quick-tempered
Quickly aroused to anger.

quiescent
Quiet, still, or inactive; tranquilly reposed.

quiet
1. An absence or near absence of agitation or activity.
2. Free of noise or uproar.

quieted
Calm or still.

quirky
Strikingly unconventional.

quixotic
Insensible about practical matters; idealistic and unrealistic.

quizzed
Examined by someone regarding knowledge about something.

quizzical
Perplexed (as if expected to know something that one does not know).

rabid
Excessively enthusiastic for and intensely devoted to a cause or idea.

racy
Full of zest or vigor.

radiant
Greatly joyful and happy.

radical
Far beyond the norm.

rage
Intense anger.

raided
Searched without warning; attacked suddenly.

railroaded
Compelled by coercion, threats, or crude means.

rambunctious
Noisy and lacking in restraint or discipline.

rancor
Deep and bitter anger and ill will.

rancorous
Having deep-seated resentment; bitter.

randy
Filled with sexual lust.

ransacked
Wrongfully stripped of anything of value.

rapacious
Excessively greedy and grasping.

rapt
In great rapture or delight.

rapture
Elated bliss.

rapturous
Happy and delighted.

rare
Uncommon in quality; especially superlative or
extreme of its kind.

rash
Defiantly disregarding danger or consequences.

rated
Measured for value, quality, effectiveness, etc.

rational
1. Consistent with reason.
2. Guided by the intellect (as distinguished from experience or emotion).

rattled
Thrown into a state of agitated confusion.

raunchy
Earthy and sexually explicit.

ravenous
Extremely hungry.

ravished
Intensely delighted; enraptured.

ravishing
Stunningly beautiful.

raw
1. Devoid of elaboration, diminution, or concealment; bare and pure.
2. Untempered and unrefined.

reachable
Easily approached.

reactionary
Opposed to political or social liberalism or reform.

reactive
Responsive to stimuli.

readiness
Prompt willingness.

ready
1. Completely prepared or in condition for immediate action, use, or progress.
2. Mentally disposed.

real
Factual or actual; having verified existence; not illusory.

realistic
Feeling aware of things as they actually are.

realization
Sudden, clear, and distinct awareness of something.

reasonable
Sound in judgment.

reassured
Restored to confidence; freed from anxiety.

rebellious
Resistant to control or authority.

reborn
1. Restored to new life and vigor.
2. Spiritually converted.

rebuffed
Bluntly rejected.

rebuked
Censured severely or angrily.

recalcitrant
Stubbornly resisting authority.

receptive
1. Open to arguments, ideas, or change.
2. Ready or willing to receive something favorably.

reckless
Defiantly disregarding danger or consequences; carelessly unconcerned.

reclusive
Withdrawn from society; seeking solitude.

recognized
1. Identified by someone or something.
2. Having a secure reputation.

reconciled
Compatible or consistent.

recovered
1. Freed from illness or injury.
2. Returned to the original or an improved state.

recreant
Abjectly fearful; cowardly.

recruited
Persuaded or sought out for employment or participation; enlisted in the military.

redeemed
1. Saved from the bondage of sin.
2. Having restored honor.

reenergized
Refreshed in vitality.

reinforced
Enhanced in strength.

refined
Having a high degree of elegance and the assurance that comes from wide social experience.

reflective
Deeply or seriously thoughtful.

refractory
Stubbornly resistant to authority or control.

refreshed
Restored of energy.

refueled
Reinvigorated with sustenance.

refused
Rejected, turned away, or declined.

regard
1. Attention to or concern for someone or something; interest.
2. Respect; relation.

regimented
Strictly controlled.

regressive
Returning to a former, less advanced state.

regret
Sadness about the loss or absence of something.

regretful
Sorrowful or feeling a sense of loss over something done or not done.

regular
1. In accordance with fixed order, procedure, or principle.
2. Not deviating from what is normal.

rejected
Rebuffed without warning.

rejection
Dismissal or refusal.

rejuvenated
Renewed in vitality or energy.

relaxed
Without strain or anxiety.

released
Free from confinement.

relentless
1. Unmoved by appeals for sympathy or forgiveness; insensible to the distresses of others; destitute of tenderness.
2. Never ceasing; persistent.

reliable
Worthy of reliance or trust.

reliant
Dependent on another for support.

relief
A lack of burdens and distress.

relieved
Free from a burden, evil, or distress.

religious
1. Believing in and reverent to a deity.
2. Extremely scrupulous and conscientious.
3. Concerned with sacred matters, religion, or the church.

relinquished
Released of possession or right.

relish
Vigorous and enthusiastic enjoyment.

reluctance
A certain degree of unwillingness.

reluctant
Unwilling, uncertain, or doubtful about something, especially something contrary to one's custom.

remarkable
1. Unusual or striking.
2. Worthy of attention because one is significant, interesting, or unusual.

reminiscent
Activating memories that are similar or suggestive of something in the past.

remiss
Failing in what duty requires.

remorseful
Feeling pain or sorrow for sins or offenses.

remorseless
Without mercy or pity.

remote
Far apart in relevance, relationship, or kinship.

removed
Separate or apart in time and/or space.

renewed
Restored to a new condition.

renowned
Widely honored and acclaimed.

repelled
Rejected outright and bluntly.

repentant
Remorseful for misdeeds.

replaceable
Capable of being substituted by someone or something else.

replaced
Removed and substituted with someone or something else.

replenished
Filled up from being empty (of sustenance, energy, etc.).

repose
Freedom from activity.

reposed
In a state of rest or sleep; tranquil.

reprehensible
Deserving of severe rebuke or censure.

repressed
Feeling the suppression of impulse or emotion.

reprimanded
Formally rebuked.

reproached
1. Criticized or mildly rebuked by someone.
2. Disgraced or shamed.

reproved
Feeling disapproval from someone; reprimanded.

repudiate
To reject or deny; to divorce.

repugnance
Intense aversion or disgust.

repugnant
Offensive to the mind.

repulsed
1. Repelled; forced or driven back.
2. Having intense distaste and aversion.

repulsive
Having the ability to repel; offensive.

rescued
Delivered from danger.

resent
Bitter displeasure or indignation.

resentment
Deep and bitter anger and ill will.

resented
Feeling bitterness from another.

resentful
Characterized by bitterness toward someone or something.

reservation
Doubt that prevents one from accepting something wholeheartedly.

reserved
Having self-restraint and reticence; slow to show emotion or opinion.

resignation
1. Acceptance of despair.
2. The sensation of giving up or letting go (as in a job or other position).

resigned
Accepting something as inevitable.

resilient
Having the ability to recover quickly.

resistance
Opposition or a resisting force from someone or something.

resistant
Impervious to being affected.

resolute
Firm in purpose or belief; determined and unwavering.

resolve
A firm purpose or belief; determination.

respect
Deep admiration and/or honor for someone or something.

respected
Deferentially regarded.

respectful
Courteous in regard and/or reverent to someone or something.

responsibility
A form of trustworthiness; the trait of being answerable to someone for something or being responsible for one's conduct.

responsible
Worthy of trust; held accountable.

responsive
Ready to react to people, events, or stimuli.

rested
Refreshed by sleeping or relaxing.

restive
Impatient, especially under restriction or delay.

restless
1. Worried and uneasy.
2. Unable to ease one's mind and/or body.

restrained
1. Reserved or using moderation; unemotional or dispassionate.
2. Restricted; deprived of free movement.

restraint
1. Limited in freedom due to a condition, rule, or other factor.
2. Controlled by someone or something.

restricted
Feeling limited in extent, number, scope, or action by someone or something.

retaliatory
Feeling justified to punish someone or something.

reticent
1. Inclined to keep silent; reserved; uncommunicative.
2. Unemotional, emotionally cool, and formal.

retired
No longer active in one's work or profession.

retiring
Reluctant to draw attention to oneself; shy.

reunited
Together again after time apart.

revengeful
Disposed to seek revenge.

revere
1. To love unquestioningly and uncritically or to excess; to venerate as an idol.
2. To have deep respect and admiration.

revered
Profoundly honored.

reverent
Having profound respect or veneration.

reviled
Criticized abusively.

revitalized
Restored to new life and vigor.

revived
Restored to consciousness, life, or vigor.

revolted
1. Filled with distaste.
2. Filled with aversion; morally offended.

revolutionary
Advocating or engaging in radical change.

revulsion
Intense aversion.

rewarded
Recognized, supported, and/or honored for something.

rich
Having an abundance of something.

ridiculed
Subject to laughter; mocked or made fun of.

ridiculous
Deserving of derision or mockery.

right
1. Free from error; especially conforming to fact or truth.
2. Morally good; justified.

righteous
Morally justified.

rigid
Fixed and unmoving; incapable of compromise or flexibility.

rigorous
1. Rigidly accurate; allowing no deviation from a standard.
2. Strict and attentive to rules and procedures.

riled
Annoyed, irritated, impatient, and/or angry.

riveted
Completely focused on and attentive to something.

robbed
Forced to part with something without consent; ripped off.

robotic
Mechanical in nature.

robust
1. Strong enough to withstand or overcome intellectual challenges or adversity.
2. Strong and sturdy.

roguish
1. Playful in a bold way.
2. Dishonest; lacking principles or scruples.

romantic
1. Soulfully or amorously idealistic.
2. Characteristic of the excitement and mystery associated with love.

rotten
1. Very bad.
2. Unsound and useless.

rough
Lacking refinement or finesse.

roused
1. Agitated or excited.
2. Awake or conscious.

rowdy
Loud and rough.

royal
Characteristic of a king or queen or a member of the king or queen's family.

rude
Lacking civility or good manners.

rueful
Feeling pain or sorrow for sins or offenses.

ruffled
Upset or disconcerted; unsettled.

ruined
1. Completely destroyed.
2. Reduced to poverty.

ruled
Subject to a ruling authority.

rushed
Pressured to do something.

ruthful
Feeling pain or sorrow for sins or offenses.

ruthless
Without mercy or pity for others; without compassion.

ruttish
Having great sexual desire.

sabotaged
Deliberately obstructed or damaged.

sacrificed
Surrendered or offered for the sake of something more desirable.

sacrificial
Included as part of a sacrifice.

sacrilegious
Grossly irreverent toward what is held to be sacred.

sad
Sorrowful or unhappy.

sadistic
Deriving pleasure or sexual gratification from inflicting pain on another.

sadness
Mournfulness and uncheerfulness.

safe
Free from danger or the risk of harm.

sagacious
Acutely insightful and wise.

sage
Wise because of age and experience.

salacious
Lustful or lecherous.

sanctified
Holy and free from sin; purified.

sanctimonious
Excessively or hypocritically pious.

sanctioned
Formally approved and invested with legal authority.

sane
Mentally healthy; free from mental disorder.

sanguine
Optimistic and/or positive.

sapient
Acutely insightful and wise.

sarcastic
Inclined to ridicule.

sardonic
Disdainfully or ironically humorous; scornful and mocking.

sassy
Improperly forward or bold.

sated
Completely satisfied.

satiated
Supplied to satisfaction.

satisfaction
Content from fulfilling a desire, need, or expectation.

satisfied
Happy and/or fulfilled.

saturnine
Heavy, slow, and gloomy; bitter or scornful.

satyr
Someone with strong sexual desire (usually a man).

saucy
1. Lightly pert and exuberant.
2. Improperly forward or bold.

savage
Extremely and violently energetic; cruelly rapacious.

saved
Rescued; especially from the power and consequences of sin.

savvy
Knowledgeable and clever about something.

scandalized
Shocked by moral violation.

scandalous
Morally offensive and injurious to someone's reputation.

scared
Fearful; frightened.

scarred
Deeply affected by pain or injury.

scathed
Injured or harmed.

scattered
Lacking orderly continuity of thoughts.

scientific
In accordance or harmony with the principles or methods used in science.

scintillating
1. Brilliantly clever.
2. Marked by high spirits or excitement.

scolded
Treated with sharp disapproval or criticism.

scorn
Intense dislike and lack of respect for a person or thing.

scorned
Treated with dislike or contempt.

scoundrelly
Lacking principles or scruples.

screwed
Defeated through trickery or deceit.

screwy
Not behaving normally.

scrutinized
Examined critically, searchingly, or in minute detail.

scurrilous
Offensively reproachful.

secondary
Lower in class, rank, or value.

secretive
Inclined to secrecy or reticence about divulging information.

secure
1. Free from fear or doubt; easy in mind.
2. Free from danger or risk.
3. Financially safe.

sedate
Dignified and somber in manner and committed to keeping promises.

sedated
Calm and quiet because of a drug or other sedative.

seduced
1. Induced to have sex.
2. Lured or enticed away from duty, principles, or proper conduct.

seductive
Attractive or enticing; sexy.

seething
Feeling intense, unexpressed anger.

seized
Taken or captured by force.

selected
Chosen in preference to another.

selective
Very careful or fastidious when making a selection.

self-absorbed
Absorbed in one's own interests or thoughts, etc.

self-acceptance
Acceptance of oneself as is—warts and all.

self-aggrandizing
Having an exaggerated sense of one's value or importance.

self-assured
Poised and having confidence in one's own worth.

self-centered
Limited to or caring only about oneself and one's own needs.

self-centeredness
Concern for one's own interests and welfare.

self-confidence
Freedom from doubt; belief in oneself and one's abilities.

self-confident
Poised and having confidence in one's own worth.

self-conscious
Excessively and uncomfortably conscious or aware of one's appearance or behavior.

self-deprecating
Critical of one's own shortcomings.

self-destructive
Dangerous to oneself or one's interests.

self-disciplined
Nonindulgent, either by nature or from personal training.

self-effacing
Reluctant to draw attention to oneself.

self-esteemed
Having respect for oneself and one's abilities.

self-expressed
Given to expression of one's individuality.

self-flagellating
Extremely critical of oneself.

self-hate
An extreme dislike or hatred of oneself.

self-indulgent
Favorably inclined to one's own appetites and desires.

selfish
Concerned chiefly or only with oneself and one's advantage to the exclusion of others.

selfless
Unselfish and concerned for the welfare of others.

selflessness
Less concern for oneself than for the success of others or of a joint activity.

self-loathing
An extreme dislike or hatred of oneself.

self-love
Excessive pride.

self-pity
Sorrow (often self-indulgent) over one's own sufferings.

self-reliant
Free from external control and constraint in, for example, action and judgment.

self-reproachful
Disappointed in or disapproving of oneself; at fault.

self-respectful
Prideful and confident in oneself; self-esteemed.

self-righteous
Excessively or hypocritically pious.

self-righteousness
Confidence in one's own righteousness.

self-sacrificing
Willing to deprive oneself.

self-serving
Interested only in oneself.

self-starting
Showing energetic initiative.

self-understanding
Able to be aware of one's own actions and responses.

senile
Infirm with age.

sensational
Cause of intense interest, curiosity, or emotion.

sensationless
Without stimuli.

sensible
Reasonable or sound in judgment.

sensitive
1. Easily offended or upset.
2. Quickly and delicately appreciative of others' feelings.

sensual
Gratifying to the senses; sexually exciting or gratifying.

sensuous
Appealing to the senses.

sentenced
Punished by someone who has judged one to be guilty of a crime.

sentimental
Tender, sad, or nostalgic.

separated
Set or kept apart from others.

serendipitous
Lucky in making unexpected and fortunate discoveries.

serene
Calm and peaceful; undisturbed; without emotional agitation.

serenity
Freedom from stress or emotion.

serious
Concerned with work or important matters rather than play or trivialities.

servile
Submissive or fawning.

set
1. Determined or decided on as by an authority.
2. Prepared and ready.

settled
Established or decided beyond dispute or doubt.

set up
Falsely charged.

sexual
Desiring or interested in sex; stimulated by sex.

sexy
Attractive or arousing sexual desire or interest; exciting or glamorous.

shadowed
Followed by someone.

shaken
Disturbed psychologically as if by a physical jolt or shock.

shaky
Insecure; beset with difficulties.

shallow
Lacking depth of intellect or knowledge; concerned only with what is obvious.

shame
Awareness of inadequacy or guilt.

shamed
Feeling a sense of guilt.

shameful
1. Deserving of disgrace.
2. Morally offensive and/or injurious to someone's reputation.

shameless
Without a sense of being disgraceful.

shaped
Influenced by someone or something.

sharp
1. Practical, hardheaded, and intelligent.
2. Clear and articulate.
3. Harsh toward another.

shattered
Ruined or disrupted.

sheepish
Timid or bashful, as though one has done something wrong.

sheltered
Protected from something bad.

shielded
Protected, hidden, or concealed from danger or harm.

shiftless
Lacking ambition or initiative; lazy.

shock
Distress and disbelief.

shocked
Struck with fear, dread, consternation, or outrage.

shook-up
Disturbed by something.

shortchanged
Deprived of something by deceit.

short-tempered
Easily aroused to anger.

shot down
Rejected by someone.

shredded
Intensely criticized.

shrewd
Practical, hardheaded, and intelligent.

shrunken
Drawn back (for example, in fear) or decreased in size, range, or extent.

shunned
Deliberately avoided.

shut out
Prevented from entering or participating in something.

shy
Lacking self-confidence.

sick
Affected by an impairment of normal function, usually by an illness or disease.

sickened
Morally offended; upset and nauseated.

sidelined
Removed from the center of activity or attention; placed into an inferior position.

significant
Rich in significance or implication.

silenced
Kept from expression, for example, by threats or pressure.

silent
Marked by absence of sound or expression.

silly
1. Ludicrous or foolish.
2. Lacking seriousness; given to frivolity.

simple
1. Lacking complexity; uncomplicated.
2. Lacking intelligence or common sense.

simplified
Simpler, easier, or reduced in complexity or extent.

sincere
Open and genuine; not deceitful.

sinful
Having a desire to commit unrighteous acts.

single
Unmarried and not attached or committed to anyone.

singled out
Selected from a group.

sinking
Uneasy or apprehensive.

skanky
Highly offensive; arousing aversion or disgust.

skeptical
Doubtful or unsure about something.

skilled
Having the capacity to perform a certain activity or task well.

skillful
Knowledgeable and apt.

skipped
Bypassed, either accidentally or on purpose.

skittish
Unpredictably excitable.

slack
A lack of rigor or strictness.

slandered
Charged falsely or with malicious intent; having one's good name and reputation attacked.

slanderous
Harmful in order to discredit or malign someone (usually through false statements).

slaphappy
1. Cheerfully irresponsible.
2. Dazed from (or as if from) repeated blows.

sleazy
Morally degraded; corrupt.

sleepless
Characterized by a lack of sleep.

sleepy
Ready to fall asleep.

slighted
Insulted or disrespected.

slimy
Morally reprehensible.

sloppy
1. With great carelessness.
2. Excessively or abnormally emotional.
3. Lacking neatness or order.

sloshed
Very drunk.

slothful
Disinclined to work; lazy.

slovenly
Negligent of neatness, especially in dress and personal hygiene; habitually dirty and unkempt.

slow
1. Lacking interest as to cause mental weariness.
2. Unintelligent or dull.

sluggish
Slow and apathetic.

sly
Cunning and deceitful.

slyness
Shrewdness as demonstrated by being skilled in deception.

small
Insignificant or unimportant; lower in rank or class.

smarmy
Unpleasantly and excessively suave or ingratiating.

smart
1. Capable of independent and intelligent action.
2. Alert, calculating, and resourceful.
3. Elegant and stylish.
4. Quick to learn.

smashed
Very drunk.

smitten
Strongly attracted to someone or something.

smooth
Agreeable and courteous with a degree of
sophistication.

smothered
1. Having little ability to move or breathe.
2. Suppressed to the point of having little or no ability
to express oneself.

smug
Excessively complacent or self-satisfied.

smugness
Excessive self-satisfaction.

snappish
Apt to speak irritably.

snappy
1. Apt to speak irritably.
2. Quick and energetic.

snarky
Disdainfully or ironically humorous; scornful and mocking.

sneaky
1. Intentionally deceptive.
2. Cautious and secretive; taking pains to avoid being observed.

snobbish
Inclined to social exclusiveness and against the advances of people considered inferior.

snobby
Inclined to social exclusiveness and against the advances of people considered inferior.

snoopy
Offensively curious or inquisitive.

snowed
Deceived by false statements.

snubbed
Rejected outright and bluntly.

snug
Comfortingly warm and/or protected.

snuggled
Drawn or pressed close to someone or something for or as if for affection or protection.

snugly
1. Fond of cuddling.
2. Safely protected.
3. Warm and comfortably sheltered.

sober
1. Not affected by a mood-altering substance, such as alcohol, an illicit drug, or medication.
2. Completely unplayful.

sociable
1. Inclined to or conducive to companionship with others.
2. Friendly and pleasant.

social
Friendly and companionable with others; enjoying activities with others.

soft
1. Tolerant or lenient.
2. Mild and pleasant.

softhearted
1. Friendly and compassionate toward others.
2. Easily moved to pity or sorrow.

soiled
Filthy or dirty.

solace
Comfort from someone or something in times of disappointment.

solaced
Morally or emotionally supported.

sold out
Revealed by another for profit and/or gain.

solemn
Dignified and somber.

solicitous
Full of anxiety and concern.

solid
1. Characterized by good, substantial quality; dependable and reliable.
2. Healthy and well-nourished.

solitary
Completely alone.

somber
Grave or gloomy.

soothed
Morally supported or emotionally strengthened by someone or something.

sophisticated
Having worldly knowledge, refinement, and savoir faire.

sordid
Morally degraded.

sore
Miserable; roused to anger.

sorrow
Grief; sadness.

sorrowful
Sad, usually because of an irreparable loss.

sorry
Regretful or sorrowful or feeling a sense of loss over something done or not done.

sound
1. Free from moral defect.
2. Financially secure and safe.

sour
Resentful, disappointed, or angry.

soured
Transitioned from finding pleasure in or approving of something to displeasure or less favorable.

spared
Saved or relieved from an experience or action.

spartan
Unsparing and uncompromising in discipline or judgment.

special
1. Unique or specific to oneself.
2. First and most important.

speechless
Temporarily incapable of speaking.

spellbound
Fixated as though by a magic spell.

spent
Depleted of energy, force, or strength.

spicy
Suggestive of sexual impropriety.

spineless
Weak in willpower, courage, or vitality.

spirited
Lively and filled with vigor.

spiritless
Having little spirit or courage; overly submissive or compliant.

spiteful
Motivated by malicious ill will and a desire to hurt.

splendid
Very good.

splendiferous
Great in beauty and splendor.

splenetic
Very irritable.

spoiled
1. Harmed by pampering or over solicitous attention.
2. Receiving extreme generosity.

spontaneous
Ready, able, and open to immediate action or response without a plan or thought of the outcome.

spooked
Frightened or scared.

sportive
Merry and frolicking.

sprightly
Full of spirit and vitality.

spry
Quick and light on the feet.

spunky
Willing to face danger; courageous.

spurned
Rejected with disdain or contempt.

squeamish
Excessively fastidious and easily disgusted.

squeezed
Feeling pressure from coercion or intimidation by someone or something.

squelched
Suppressed by force.

stable
Firm and dependable; subject to little fluctuation.

staid
Dignified and proper.

stained
Damage to one's reputation.

stale
Lacking originality or spontaneity.

stalked
Followed and obsessively harassed by someone or something.

startled
Excited by sudden surprise or alarm.

starved
Extremely hungry; suffering from lack of food.

static
Stable with little change.

steadfast
Firm and dependable, especially in loyalty.

steady
Firm in determination or resolution; not shakable.

stereotyped
Categorized or judged unwarrantedly.

sterile
1. Incapable of reproducing.
2. Deficient in originality or creativity; lacking powers of invention.

stern
Severe and unremitting in making demands.

stew
To be agitated; to worry.

stewing
Fraught with extreme worry and agitation.

stiff
1. Rigidly formal.
2. Firm in determination or resolution; not shakable.
3. Very drunk.

stifled
Suppressed or constrained.

stigmatized
Marked with disgrace.

still
Silent and calm without movement.

stilted
Artificially formal.

stimulated
Alert and energetic; having stirred emotions.

stingy
Unwilling to spend (money, time, resources, etc.).

stirred
Excited or provoked to the expression of an emotion; emotionally aroused.

stodgy
Excessively conventional and unimaginative and, hence, dull.

stoic
Unaffected by pleasure or pain; impassive.

stolid
Showing little emotion or sensibility; not easily aroused or excited.

stoned
Under the influence of narcotics.

stonewalled
1. Obstructed, delayed.
2. Lacking cooperation from someone.

stout
Dependable and/or inured to fatigue or hardships.

stouthearted
Courageous and dependable.

strained
Lacking natural ease; mentally and emotionally tense.

stranded
Cut off or left behind.

strange
Out of the ordinary and unexpected; slightly odd or a bit weird.

strangled
1. Held in check with difficulty.
2. Choked by someone or something.

strength
Power from being physically and/or mentally strong.

strengthened
Made stronger by someone or something.

stressed
Pressured or strained.

stretched
Extended to a physical or mental limit.

stricken
Grievously affected, especially by disease.

strict
Severe and unremitting in making demands.

striving
Effortfully attempting to attain a goal.

stroked
Treated gingerly or carefully.

strong
Having strength or power greater than average or expected.

struck
Affected by something overwhelming.

stubborn
Tenaciously unwilling or marked by tenacious unwillingness to yield.

stuck
Fixed on something and unable to move; baffled.

studious
Taking care and effort with something. Often relates to studying or pursuits of knowledge.

stuffed
Filled with something.

stumped
Perplexed or confounded.

stung
Aroused to impatience or anger.

stunned
Senseless or dizzy; overwhelmingly surprised or shocked.

stunted
Inferior in size or quality.

stupefied
Struck dumb with astonishment and surprise.

stupendous
Awesome because of greatness in size, force, or extent.

stupid
1. Lacking intellectual acuity; mentally numb.
2. Lacking intelligence.

stuporous
Stunned or confused and slow to react.

sturdy
Confident and determined.

stylish
Elegant or tasteful or refined in manners or dress.

suave
Smoothly agreeable and courteous with a degree of sophistication.

subdued
Quiet and reflective; depressed.

subjected
Subservient; forced to submit to someone or something; dominated or influenced.

subjugated
Put down by force or intimidation; subservient.

sublime
Adored or revered; awe-inspiring.

submissive
Inclined or willing to submit to the orders or wishes of others.

subordinate
Lower in rank or importance.

subordinated
Made subordinate, dependent, or subservient.

subservient
Compliant and obedient to authority.

substantial
Considerable in importance, size, or worth.

subtle
Difficult to detect or grasp by the mind or analyze.

subversive
Opposing a civil authority or government.

successful
Having reached a desired goal; marked by a favorable outcome.

suffering
Misery and/or pain.

suffocated
Stultified, suppressed, or stifled.

suggestive
Compelled to suggest or imply something.

suicidal
1. Dangerous to oneself or one's interests.
2. Having the intention to kill oneself.

sulk
To show sullen aloofness or withdrawal; to show displeasure.

sulky
Sullen or moody.

sullen
Lonely; solitary; desolate.

sullied
Placed under suspicion or charged falsely.

sunk
Doomed to extinction.

sunny
Bright and pleasant.

super
Of the highest quality; excellent.

superb
Beyond excellent.

supercilious
Arrogantly superior to and disdainful of those one views as unworthy.

superficial
Concerned with or comprehending only what is apparent or obvious; not deep or penetrating emotionally or intellectually.

superior
1. High in rank or importance.
2. Above being affected or influenced by someone or something.

superseded
Replaced by someone.

superstitious
Ignorant of the laws of nature and having faith in magic or chance.

support
Assistance, help, or aid with something.

supported
Strengthened or assisted by the moral or psychological aid or encouragement of someone or something.

supportive
Giving sympathy or encouragement to someone or something.

suppressed
Restrained; held back.

sure
Without doubt or uncertainty; confident and assured.

surly
Inclined to anger or bad feelings with overtones of menace.

surpassed
Overcome and/or passed by someone or something.

surprise
Astonishment and wonder from something totally
unexpected happening to oneself.

surreal
Resembling a dream; fantastic in imagery and
incongruous juxtapositions.

surrender
Acceptance of despair.

surrendered
Having relinquished possession or control over.

surveyed
Considered in a comprehensive way.

susceptible
Easily impressed emotionally.

suspended
1. Rendered temporarily ineffective.
2. Temporarily barred from something.

suspicious
Openly distrustful and unwilling to confide.

swamped
Overwhelmed by something.

sweet
Pleasant and kind.

swell
Very good.

swindled
Deprived of something by deceit.

sycophantic
Excessively attentive in order to gain advantage.

sympathetic
Having sympathy, compassion, or friendliness.

sympathy
A shared feeling with others (especially feelings of sorrow or anguish).

synergistic
Cooperative and collaborative with others for an enhanced effect.

systematic
Methodical in process or approach in doing something.

tacky
Tastelessly showy.

tactful
Having a sense of what is fitting and considerate in dealing with others.

tainted
Affected by something bad or corrupt.

talented
Endowed with a skill or skills.

talkative
Friendly, open, and willing to talk.

talky
Full of trivial conversation.

tame
Very restrained or quiet; docile.

tantalized
Harassed with persistent criticism or harping.

tarnished
Dishonored or disgraced.

tasty
Feeling pleasing to the senses.

taut
Subjected to great tension.

taxed
Lacking energy; depleted.

tearful
Filled with strong sadness, joy, or other strong, tear-invoking emotion.

teased
1. Mildly pleasurably excited.
2. Annoyed or bothered.

temperamental
Subject to sharply varying moods.

temperate
Characterized by moderation in behavior.

tempted
Provoked by someone to do something through (often false or exaggerated) promises or persuasion.

tenacious
Stubbornly unyielding.

tender
Sympathetic, gentle, or sentimental.

tenderness
Warmth and affection.

tense
Unable to relax; nervous, anxious.

tentative
Unsettled in mind or opinion; hesitant.

tenuous
Lacking substance or significance.

tepid
Having little interest or enthusiasm.

terrible
Intensely or extremely bad or unpleasant.

terrific
Very great or intense.

terrified
Extremely fearful or in a state of terror.

terror
Overwhelming fear and anxiety.

terrorized
Coerced by violence or with threats.

testy
Easily irritated or annoyed.

thankful
Grateful and appreciative.

thirsty
Extremely desirous, usually of water or fluids.

thoughtful
Considerate of the feelings or well-being of others.

threatened
Endangered and vulnerable.

thrifty
Careful and diligent in the use of resources.

thrilled
Intensely and pleasurably excited.

thunderstruck
Struck dumb with astonishment and surprise.

thwarted
Hindered or prevented from the success of efforts, plans, or desires.

ticked
Upset, agitated, or angry.

tickled
Pleased or joyous.

tight
1. Lacking generosity.
2. Very drunk.
3. Demanding of strict attention to rules and procedures.

timid
Fearful and cautious; insecure.

timorous
Lacking confidence; nervous.

tired
Depleted of strength or energy.

tolerance
The willingness to recognize and respect the beliefs or practices of others.

tolerant
1. Respectful of the rights, opinions, or practices of others.
2. Forgiving under provocation.
3. Open-minded.

tormented
Mental suffering from disturbing thoughts or from the provocation of others.

torn
Disrupted by the pull of contrary forces.

torpid
Slow and apathetic; lethargic.

tortured
In intense pain.

touched
Affected emotionally.

touchy
Oversensitive; irritable or quick to anger.

tough
1. Strong and determined.
2. Capable of enduring hardship.

tragic
Very sad; especially involving grief, death, or destruction.

tranquil
Calm and serene.

transformed
Changed or altered in form, appearance, or nature.

transported
1. Spellbound by someone or something.
2. Feeling as if in another place and/or time.
3. Overwhelmed from an emotion.

trapped
Placed in a confining or embarrassing position.

trashed
1. Very drunk.
2. Ridiculed or highly criticized.

treacherous
Dangerously unstable and unpredictable.

treasured
Held dear; highly valued.

tremendous
Extreme in degree, extent, amount, or impact.

trenchant
Clearly or sharply defined in the mind.

trepidation
Alarm or dread; fear of something that may happen.

tricked
Fooled by deceit.

trickery
Deception intended to take advantage.

triumph
Ecstatic with joy from a successful ending of a struggle or contest.

triumphant
Joyful and proud, especially because of triumph or success.

troubled
Distressed or anxious.

truculent
Defiantly aggressive.

true
1. Consistent with fact or reality; not false.
2. Authentic and genuine.
3. Devoted (sometimes fanatically) to a cause or concept or to truth.

trust
1. Complete confidence in someone or something.
2. Belief in the honesty and reliability of others.
3. Certainty based on past experience.

trusted
Worthy of trust or confidence.

trustworthy
Responsible for one's conduct and obligations.

truthful
Filled with honesty; honest.

turmoil
A violent disturbance or agitation.

turned on
Filled with enthusiasm and pleasure.

two-faced
Deceptive and insincere.

tyrannized

1. Oppressively governed.
2. Treated cruelly by someone or something in absolute power or control.

ugly
Displeasing to the senses; unpleasant.

umbrage
Anger caused by being offended.

unable
Lacking the necessary physical or mental ability to do something.

unaccepted
Rejected; not accepted.

unacknowledged
Ignored; not recognized or admitted.

unafraid
Oblivious to dangers or perils or calmly resolute in facing them; feeling no fear.

unaggressive
Not aggressive; not given to fighting or assertiveness.

unappreciated
Feeling lack of acknowledgment of one's value.

unashamed
Without shame.

unassuming
Without arrogance or presumption.

unassured
Lacking confidence.

unattached
Free from emotional attachment to someone or something.

unattractive
Unappealing to the senses.

unbalanced
Out of balance spiritually, physically, mentally, or emotionally.

unburdened
Free from difficulties or responsibilities.

uncanny
Suggestive of supernatural influences; mysterious.

uncaring
Lacking affection or compassion.

uncertain
Lacking confidence or assurance.

unchivalrous
Offensively discourteous.

unclear
Causing confusion and/or doubt.

uncomfortable
Causing mental discomfort.

uncommitted
Free and available.

uncompromising
Unwilling to make concessions to others.

unconcerned
Lacking interest or uncaring.

unconfident
Insecure and/or hesitant.

unconfined
Free from confinement or restraint.

unconscious
Not conscious; lacking awareness and the capacity for sensory perception, as if asleep or dead.

unconstrained
Free from being held or controlled by someone or something.

uncontrollable
Incapable of being controlled or managed.

unconvinced
Lacking conviction.

unconvincing
Unable to inspire belief.

undaunted
Resolutely courageous; unshaken in purpose.

undecided
Open and uncommitted; subject to further thought.

underestimated
Perceived to be or to have less of something (such as an ability) than what one actually possesses.

undergirded
Morally supported.

understanding
Comprehension, discernment, and empathy.

understood
Perceived and comprehended by others.

underwhelmed
Unimpressed and disappointed.

undeserving
Not deserving or worthy of something.

undesirable
1. Not worthy of being chosen.
2. Not wanted.

undone
Thrown into a state of disorganization or incoherence.

uneasy
Discomforted; anxious.

unemotional
Unsusceptible to or destitute of emotion or feelings.

unenthusiastic
Lacking excitement or ardor.

unequal
Poorly balanced or matched.

uneven
Not fairly matched as opponents.

unexcited
Not excited.

unfaltering
Firmly determined or resolute; not shakable.

unfamiliar
Not known or not well-known.

unfeeling
Devoid of feeling for others; devoid of sensation.

unfettered
Free from restraint; unbound.

unfit
Lacking qualification or in bad or unsuitable condition.

unflinching
Brave in the face of danger.

unforgiving
Unwilling or unable to forgive or show mercy.

unfortunate
Not favored by fortune; marked or accompanied by or resulting in ill fortune.

unfriendly
Feeling not disposed to friendship or friendliness.

unfulfilled
Lacking satisfaction.

ungratified
Worried and uneasy.

unhampered
Not slowed, blocked, or interfered with.

unhappy
Sad, sorrowful, or discontented; not happy; miserable.

unhealthy
Poor in health of body or mind.

unhinged
1. Uneasy, worried, or alarmed.
2. Affected with madness or insanity.

unimpeded
Free from obstruction or hindrance.

unimpressed
Without admiration, respect, or interest; unmoved to serious regard.

uninformed
Not informed; lacking in knowledge or information.

uninhibited
Free from inhibition or restraint.

uninspired
Without intellectual, emotional, or spiritual excitement.

unintelligent
Lacking intelligence.

uninterested
Without care or interest in knowing.

uninteresting
Boring, dull, or unimaginative.

uninviting
Neither attractive nor tempting.

unique
Radically distinctive and without equal.

united
Joined into a single entity.

unity
An undivided or unbroken completeness or totality, with nothing wanting.

unjust
Not equitable or fair.

unknown
Not known, not famous, or not acclaimed.

unlovable
Incapable of inspiring love or affection.

unloved
Not loved.

unlucky
Misfortune seemingly brought on by chance rather than by one's own actions.

unmotivated
Lacking inspiration, interest, or enthusiasm to do something.

unmoved
Calm and emotionally unshaken.

unneeded
Not necessary.

unnerved
Deprived of courage and strength.

unnoticed
Not acknowledged, observed, or identified.

unobstructed
Free from impediment, obstruction, or hindrance.

unostentatious
Unpretentious and having good taste.

unpleasant
Offensive or disagreeable; causing discomfort or unhappiness.

unpredictable
Given to unexpected or erratic behavior.

unpretentious
Lacking pretension or affection; restrained with good taste.

unrecognized
Unknown or not having a secure reputation.

unreliable
Not worthy of reliance or trust.

unresentful
Not resentful; compassionate and/or forgiving.

unrestrained
Characterized by uncontrolled excitement or emotion.

unromantic
Neither expressive of nor exciting sexual love or romance.

unruffled
Free from emotional agitation or nervous tension.

unruly
Unwilling to submit to authority.

unsafe
Lacking security or safety.

unsated
Not having been satisfied.

unsatisfied
Lacking fulfillment.

unseemly
Improper or inappropriate.

unsettled
Disturbed; in doubt; lacking stability.

unsexy
Lacking sexual arousal or sexual attraction.

unshackled
Liberated; free and without restraint.

unshakable
Firm in determination or resolution; not shakable.

unsparing
1. Very generous.
2. Unmerciful and ruthless.

unstable
1. Suffering from severe mental illness.
2. Without ease or reassurance.
3. Subject to change; variable.

unsure
Lacking confidence or assurance.

unsuspecting
Without suspicion; unaware.

unusual
Out of the ordinary and unexpected; slightly odd or a bit weird.

unwanted
Not needed or desired.

unwavering
Firm in determination or resolution; not shakable.

unwelcome
Not welcome; not giving pleasure or not received with pleasure.

unwise
Lacking judgment or wisdom.

unworthy
1. Undeserving; lacking in value or merit.
2. Morally reprehensible.

unyielding
Stubbornly determined and purposeful.

up
Ready, optimistic, and/or energized.

upbeat
In a contented state of being happy, healthy, and prosperous.

uplifted
Exalted emotionally, especially with pride.

upset
Angry; unhappy, sad, or disappointed.

uptight
Tense with anxiety or anger.

used
Taken advantage of by someone or something.

useless
Without beneficial use or incapable of functioning usefully.

usurped
Without control (over personal rights, for example) without authority and possibly with force.

vacant
Devoid of intelligence or thought.

vacillation
Indecision in speech or action.

vague
Lacking clarity or distinctness.

vain
Characterized by false pride; having an exaggerated sense of self-importance.

valiant
Courageous and determined; having valor.

valid
Well grounded in logic or truth or having legal force.

validated
Declared or made legally valid.

valor
Heroic courage.

valorous
With valor; exceptionally or heroically courageous when facing danger.

valued
Highly regarded or in esteem for admirable qualities, especially of an intrinsic nature.

vapid
Lacking significance, liveliness, spirit, or zest.

vehement
Characterized by intensity of emotions or conviction.

venerate
To respect and show reverence.

venery
Desire for sexual pleasure or indulgence.

vengeful
Disposed to seek revenge or intended for revenge.

venturesome
Disposed to venture or taking risks.

verve
Energy; vitality.

vexed
Troubled persistently; annoyed.

vicious
Having deep ill will; deliberately harmful, cruel, and/or violent.

victimized
Exploited; taken advantage of; angry and/or pained due to cruelty or unjust treatment from others.

vigorous
Forceful and energetic in action or activity.

villainous
Extremely wicked.

vindictive
Characterized by malicious ill will and a desire to hurt; motivated by spite.

violent
Displaying a great force or energy or extreme emotional intensity.

virulent
Hostile; harsh or corrosive.

vitalized
Lively or vigorous.

vivacious
Vigorous and animated.

volatile
Erratically changeable in affections or attachments; liable to lead to sudden change or violence.

voracious
Excessively greedy and grasping.

wallow
To feel unrestrained indulgence.

want
Desire for someone or something.

wanton
Sexually immodest or promiscuous.

warm
Friendly and responsive; affectionate.

warmhearted
Sympathetic and kind.

wary
Keenly cautious, watchful, and prudent.

weak-kneed
Lacking power or resolution.

weary
Fatigued or strained.

weepy
Tearful; inclined to weep.

well-meaning
With good intentions.

wicked
1. Morally bad in principle or practice.
2. Naughtily or annoyingly playful.

wild
Extremely lacking in restraint or control.

willful
With deliberate intention.

wishful
Having desire for something.

wistful
Pensive and sad.

withdrawn
Detached or pulled back from active participation.

woeful
Grieving; sorrowful or miserable.

wonder
1. Surprised and/or astonished by something curious or unknown.
2. Doubt or uncertainty about something.

worried
Distressed; anxious and uneasy, troubled, or grieving.

worship
To love and admire profoundly; to be devoted.

wrathful
Intensely angry.

wretched
Very unhappy; miserable.

XYZ

xenophobic
Abnormally afraid or hateful of the strange or foreign.

yearn
To strongly desire.

yearning
Prolonged unfulfilled desire or need.

yeasty
Spirited and joyful.

yen
A yearning for something or to do something.

zealous
Enthusiastically interested.

zestful
Spirited and joyful.

NOTES

The online version of WordNet served as the primary source for the common-use definitions provided. [Princeton University "About WordNet." WordNet. Princeton University. 2010. http://wordnet.princeton.edu]

Common-use words and definitions for feelings, moods, and emotions were also evaluated through Google Search and the sources listed below.

Andrews, Synthia. "Chapter 7." In *The Path of Emotions: Transform Emotions into Energy to Achieve Your Greatest Potential*, 86-87. Pompton Plains, NJ: New Page Books, 2013.

"The Comprehensive Alphabetical List of Emotions." The Emotion Identifier: Find the Words. http://idyouremotions.com/.

Dictionary.com. http://dictionary.reference.com/.

Merriam-Webster's Collegiate Dictionary. Springfield, MA: Merriam-Webster, 2003.

Webster, Noah. "Webster's 1913 Dictionary." Online Dictionary. http://www.webster-dictionary.org/.

Whelan, Jeremy. "Dictionary Of The Emotions." In *Mosaic Acting System: A Bold Approach to Acting & Directing*. Calif.: Whelan International, 2004.

"Wiktionary." Wiktionary. http://www.wiktionary.org/.

ABOUT THE AUTHOR

Patrick Michael Ryan is the founder and CEO of PAMAXAMA. He has served in leadership roles for companies representing a range of industries, including real estate, retreading, fitness, and web development. His experience includes several years of working as a professional actor and in various production roles for theatre, television, film, and radio. Patrick studied acting at the California Institute of the Arts. He lives in Portland, Oregon with his wife and 2 children.

www.dictionaryofemotions.com

Made in the USA
Middletown, DE
11 November 2018